7 FIGURE FAITH

A BIBLICAL APPROACH TO MASTERING THE MARKETPLACE, AS A WOMAN OF INFLUENCE CALLED TO MILLIONS

By

TAUSHAUNA BURREL

7-FIGURE FAITH: A BIBLICAL APPROACH TO MASTERING THE MARKETPLACE, AS A WOMAN OF INFLUENCE CALLED TO MILLIONS

ISBN: 979-8-9892806-4-3
Library of Congress Control Number: 2024909265

Published by 120 Publishing House.
5240 Prairie View Way, Wesley Chapel FL 33545
www.120dayspublishing.com

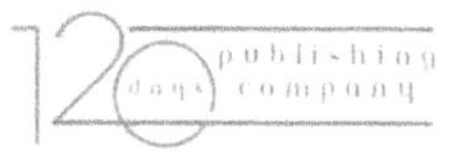

HELLO WOMAN OF FAITH!

Welcome to the journey!

Hi there! I'm Taushauna Burrel, a marketplace Apostle of the Lord, but you can call me Peach! I've been commissioned and sent to rebuild cities and wastelands and to announce God's prophetic voices and apostles as we navigate these thrilling end times. My calling? To empower women like you to boldly step into the mantle of your life, whether that's lighting up the marketplace or nurturing an impactful ministry right from your home.

I'm the proud founder of 120 Publishing House, an Elite Media Agency, where we champion Christian women called to spread their prophetic messages across nations—from stages to the pages of their books. We're all about transforming ministers into moguls, helping you craft a message that not only reaches millions but also creates a massive impact, all while supporting the Kingdom's call on your life.

Together with my husband and our 5 children, I also steer Lender Not Borrower International Ministries. Here, we're weaving a network of God's leaders and Kingdom builders, committed to spreading the Gospel and reigniting the power of prayer globally. We're creating homes of prayer all over the world, turning every nook and cranny into a sanctuary of faith.

It's an absolute joy to be in this place, doing what I love and fulfilling my purpose—and I tell you, none of this would have been possible without activating my faith and saying 'yes' to a life of 7-figure impact, both in the marketplace and beyond. So, are you ready to dive in?

Great!

And hey, I've got a little something extra for you—click the link below for a special invite to join our vibrant Facebook community of 7 Figure Faith'ers. It's a place buzzing with energy, support, and inspiration. Plus, you'll get the chance to win in our monthly giveaways for new members and even be part of our annual $1,000 draw for our winner and a charity of their choice.

Can't wait to see you there!

Click or copy the link below to join us, or scan the QR code beneath
Join Our Facebook Community
https://www.facebook.com/groups/7figurefaithers

Taushauna "AP" Burrel, The Manuscript Midwife

DEDICATION

This book is dedicated to every woman who has ever dared to dream beyond her circumstances, to those called to carry the mantle of influence and affluence in the marketplace.

To the silent warriors shaping futures through prayer, and the bold visionaries who build bridges where there were once barriers.

May your faith always be the beacon that guides you to your divine destination.

CONTENTS

PREFACE

This is a book idea that God gave me during the most financially dependent seasons of my life. My family of 7 was living with a neighbor. We were surviving on state assistance, while running a new online ministry from our car, and building a publishing company from our local library. I still have prayer videos on my YouTube page of me in the car recording them because I had nowhere to film in the neighbor's home while we lived there.

I remember reminding God of all the things He had spoken to me, about who I was daily through my affirmations. I would say this daily.

"Good morning Jesus, it's me, I am Taushauna Burrel, Kingdom Ambassador and Wealth Distribution Center for Kingdom advancement and initiatives. I am called to millions, I have a message for the masses, and my mandate will be made manifest in the Earth, with the help of God and my God-given SHIPS! I speak to every ship that carries cargo for my destiny!

I have the right relationSHIPS, friendSHIPS, MentorShips, PartnerSHIPS, and LeaderSHIP, to take me from now to my next! I travel the world teaching people the principles of wealth and success. My family is blessed, my husband is blessed and his name is known at the gates of great rooms. Together we travel with our family teaching people the principles of success. I drive a white Range Rover, with license plate Blessed PG, I own a black BMW, and a Yacht named God's Glory. I am blessed and everything I touch prospers. The angels of the Lord are ready to assist me in all that I do and the favor of the Lord follows me. I have grown in wisdom and stature, and the favor of men follows and goes before me too! My obstacles are moving out of my way, and everything I want wants me back. Nothing is in the way, and everything I need is on the way. My billions are in my belief. Therefore I believe that I have them now! I receive them now. I am a generous giver and also a generous receiver. I am called to wealth and to impact the nations and today is going to be a great day."

I said so much more that I will get into later in this book, but the point is I understand the power of faith, and what activates faith. Despite my current circumstances, I was determined not to let those situations prophesy my future. In other words, my circumstances were not the reality I chose to believe. I had decided that I would only operate in the faith that would activate my millions. And that faith is what carried me to my 7 million dollar year! Whoa! That's prophetic. I don't even know why I wrote that other than that it is a principle in action, and God intended for me to say 7 million dollars a year, because as I write this, I have yet to accomplish that yet, but now, I know it's on the way.

How do I know that, and how can I make such a bold statement you might ask? Well, that's what this book is all about. This book is about sharing with you the very principles of faith, leadership, and vision that I activated and executed in the year God told me I would become a millionaire, and I finally decided to believe it.

While the idea of this book was born in a place that spoke to lack, the urgency to finally write it came from a prophetic push of radical obedience while I was in a spiritual, mental, physical, and financial place of abundance. I wasn't quite a millionaire financially yet, but the word was spoken, and I knew all too well how accurate God was when I matched my faith with His promise! Thus 7-Figure Faith was BIRTHED!

So what in the world is 7-Figure Faith?

7 Figure Faith is the faith for MILLIONS! It is the faith necessary to walk in the mantle of millions, catapulted by the consistent application of everyday disciplines, biblical principles, and miraculous thinking.

So whether you are called to impact millions, accumulate and distribute millions of dollars, or both, this book is for you. However, the person that this will truly ignite and activate are those who KNOW that millions in impact and influence is their portion. If this is you, then you are looking for biblical backing and guidance on your road to securing this very real fate for you.

This is not another book of washed-down and commercialized prosperity gospel rhetoric

First of all the Gospel, all by itself is the most prosperous teaching of all the world. However, people and the name it and claim it, all faith and no work, Jesus the Genie in the bottle, charismatic teaching with no sustenance, has made it hard for people to believe that God, Jesus, truly wants us to not just prosper, but to prosper and be a blessing to nations. It's the very essence of our Abrahamic covenant, when we were redeemed we were redeemed to be a great nation, to be blessed, and a blessing to many nations. However, that requires FAITH and ACCEPTANCE, along with a relationship that will guide you towards the plans to prosper you as God promised.

Abraham had God directly as a guide when his faith wavered, we, the children of this covenant, have access to the Holy Ghost, and His teachings and principles to guide us when we need added help. This help and these principles unlock the mysteries of impacting and influencing nations to advance the Kingdom and to allow you to live a life more abundantly than what was offered before our new covenant with Christ. In this book, I lay out some of those principles, along with a guide, that God gave me. It's my 7-step framework, called COMPASS and I lead you through these principles to increase your faith to 7-Figure Faith, as you read along.

The Compass Guide to this book

Each of the final 7 chapters in this book is broken down into an overarching principle that Highlights a part of your "C.O.M.P.A.S.S" to millions. Within each chapter, I share my story, and practical bible based teachings to help you better understand how to apply that principle to your life, and then at the end of the chapter we put what we have learned into action. So we have principles of faith, and then we take action in our Faith It Now section at the end of each chapter. For added accountability, I had throughout the book exercises you can also share in our Facebook community.

Finally, there are parts in this book filled with quotes, prayers, or a deeper understanding of certain topics. I call these "Power Pauses". These are times you can pause to study the thought or just put a pin in it and come back to it at a later time.

My Promise to You

I wrote this book out of obedience, so I can promise you that the words written are coming from me, under the guidance of the Holy Spirit. This is a book that will not only develop your faith but will make you a better person, and more effective leader in the marketplace, your home, and ministry. I promise you that you will gain at least one, life-altering nugget or revelation from reading this book.

Walk with me as we dialogue, walkthrough, breakthrough, and live out the mustard seed principles needed to operate in

7 figure faith to seize the wealth and the abundance that God has called you to.

No need to take notes, this is a book about taking action, so at the end of each chapter I have an action step I want you to take and for accountability, you can join our private group of future millionaires, multi-millionaires, deca-millionaires, and billionaires, that are on this journey of operating in this type of faith too. Join us here now, and share your name, and what you are in expectation of after this book is complete. At the end of each chapter will be a hashtag of accountability that you can use to identify your progress on your journey!

God bless you, and enjoy this journey because life is about to take a major turn for the better!

Taushauna Burrel

INTRODUCTION

This book was almost called The 6-figure Year. I know, I know. If you know me as a publisher, you would have been very disappointed, because it was just a whack title. I was only excited because the testimony I had receipts for, was actually playing out the way God said it would , and so I knew I would write this book, but had no idea that it would be THIS BOOK!

So what do you mean Peach? Oh, my bad, I forgot to mention, that although many around the world know me as Taushauna The Manuscript Midwife, or Apostle Peach, the international orator, marketplace activator, and mantle igniter for Christ; my closest friends and family members call me Peach. It's a childhood nickname that stayed with me, my entire life. Literally, as a collegiate basketball player and national champion, I would get announced as Peaches Churchwell, as if that was my first name.

So, since we are on this ride together, I will be allowing you into my most intimate financial stories, and faith-filled stories, and even push you to share some of yours; You can now call me Peach if I ever see you out in these Kingdom streets :-) Chile we just became besties real quick.

Ok, back to the good stuff.

So in writing this book, I was under the misconception that God wanted me to write about what He was currently doing in my life, but in fact, like true God-fashion, He wanted to write a book about the future. Your future, and how to make your future a RIGHT NOW REALITY.

This is a book to prepare you for what God has already prepared for you, but there is a disconnect in the process and it is the fulfillment of carrying out laws and principles through understanding and knowledge.

The greatest book I have ever read says that people perish for a lack of knowledge, and in all your ways you should seek to understand. So while many people are indeed equipped with faith and truly believe God will get them to the abundant life He has promised, they fail to realize that it is the partnership with principles and practices that makes that faith come alive. Simply put, faith without works is indeed dead, but what is the work? That's the application of the principles that we will release in this book, along with a hefty prayer life, and partnership with God no matter the circumstances.

So walk with me as we uncover what 7 figure Faith is, what it looks like in action, and my 7-step framework and the biblical principles that will lead you into tapping into a 7-figure year and beyond. I am going to show you how my guide, The 7-Figure Faith C.O.M.P.A.S.S.©, is critical for anyone looking to transition from a place of limiting faith to a proclamation of abundance

THE 7-FIGURE FAITH C.O.M.P.A.S.S©

CHAPTER 1: THE RULE OF REST

2021 was a pivotal year for me—a year where the grind of entrepreneurship met the grace of God-given rest. At eight months pregnant, leading a network marketing team that fluctuated between 75 to 200 spirited individuals, I was at the peak of my game. Imagine that—orchestrating a massive team, all while navigating the highs and lows of network marketing. This was no job for the faint-hearted; it was a proving ground for resilience, leadership, and integrity.

Just as I was gearing up for another growth sprint before my maternity leave, God pressed the pause button on my plans. Instead of pushing harder, He whispered, "Rest." This wasn't just about taking a break; it was about learning to operate in a kingdom manner, where business aligns with biblical peace, not worldly pressure.

Rest, sounded like a curse word to me, with the way I was so addicted to toiling! I ignored that message so fast because surely this was not God. Or so I thought.

At 34 weeks pregnant, overwhelmed, and underpaid, I was orchestrating 3-5 Zoom meetings, managing a sprawling team, and keeping up with the demanding travel that my role required. It was during a late-night call, my soul weary and voice nearly broken, that my closest allies Sharonda and Jonahl said to me:

> *"Peach, you can't do this anymore, and don't even think about traveling to Houston next month because we know you!"*

I don't know if it was in their tone or their eyes as we sat on that zoom call, but all I could feel was the word God had spoken days earlier... It was time to Rest. Tears began to flow from my eyes and I realized that my hustle and grind was more than about getting to a bag, it revealed my faith in toiling and expecting that I was the only one who could provide for me.

I realized that this moment was not just a plea for sympathy but a divine intervention. God's directive was clear and succinct—Rest. Little did I know, God was setting the stage for me to truly begin to understand how the marketplace in the Kingdom Economy worked.

The REST of God

One of my favorite teachers and mentors from afar, Pastor Gary Kesee of Faith Life Now, teaches that rest is a covenant with God—it's a promise that when we honor His rhythms and His sabbath, He honors our needs. Rest is a liberation from the curse of endless labor and toil that Adam's fall from grace introduced us to, and when we accept God's rest, it becomes a redemptive call to align with the Abrahamic covenant (new covenant), that Christ restored us back to when He introduced grace back into our lives.

> *... cursed is the ground because of you; through painful toil, you will eat food from it all the days of your life" (Genesis 3:17, New International Version)*
>
> *And if you are Christ's, then you are Abraham's offspring, heirs according to promise. Galatians 3:29*

God's instruction to rest reshaped my understanding of work and success. It wasn't about stopping but about aligning my work with His plans and understanding this principle for what was next. By stepping back, I allowed God to step in, doubling my team's size, and skyrocketing my business achievements without my direct hand. This was the miracle of divine rest—prosperity and promotions that came not from toil but from trust.

The Principle of Rest

The principle of rest, deeply rooted in the law of the Sabbath, commands us to cease work one day a week, recognizing and reverencing God's order. This obedience resets our spiritual compass, aligns us with God's provisions, and refreshes our soul and soil for the upcoming tasks. Ignoring this divine directive not only disrespects God's design but slowly erodes our vitality, paving a path to burnout and spiritual barrenness.

However, embracing this Sabbath rest as I did, even amidst financial turbulence and entrepreneurial demands, opened a floodgate of blessings and operational ease. It realigned my efforts with God's effortless provision, turning my minimal input into maximum output—a true testament to the power of resting in God. Rest sharpens our focus, invigorates our spirit, and multiplies our efforts by divine magnitudes. It is not inaction; it is a heavenly orchestrated action that positions us for greater victories and sustainable success.

The Types of Rest Available to You

One thing I learned on my journey before the revelation of 7-figure faith, is that it is easy to place revenue over rest, and then wonder why burnout is our portion and not blessings.

It's simply because we sowed seeds of labor during the seasons of rest, and the harvest of overworking will always be burdens that show up in our health, mental health, or financial health.

However, when a person taps into the rest principle, even with just mustard seed faith, they will begin to reap the benefits of a level head, and a peaceful mind, and begin to enjoy peaceful profits.

The season of rest God gave me was a season of physical, mental, and spiritual rest. This was crucial for me because, for years, I had neglected to allow myself to rest in these areas adequately. I needed to understand and practice this principle before walking into abundance. Not resting was actually upholding my abundance. When I understood that I became intentional about resting. Now did I get it right, 100% of the time after this unique experience, no? But I did develop a sense of yielding that would be necessary for what was coming next.

Now as I grow, I understand that as a business owner and woman trusted with a mantle in the marketplace, I must rest and learn how to develop leaders around me so that I can rest from my business and as well as do the same in the home with adequately developing my children so that I am not burnt out there either. Just know that rest is a requirement at every level, and the strategy shifts, but the principle remains. Before we can tap into 7-Figure Faith, we have to understand resting and its power.

There is no need to even attempt the rest of what's offered in these pages if you don't commit to this principle now.

A Deeper Look at Rest

The Bible is clear on the benefits of Rest. When we follow God's commandment for us to rest, it restores and blesses us.

There are 3 major benefits of Rest when God says so.

1. It allows God to provide for us supernaturally (Exodus 16:23–30). But we have to make the decision to trust in His provision.
2. It also allows us to rest and be refreshed (Exodus 31:14–17).
3. There is safety and protection in Rest. (Psalm 91)

There are also consequences when we do not rest.

1. Numbers 15:32–36; 2 Chronicles 36:20–21
2. We must remember that there is a principle of life and death behind every one of the Ten Commandments.
3. We could be slowly killing ourselves by not resting one day a week.

There are blessings when we rest.

1. Mark 2:23–28 The Sabbath is a gift to us from God. It is meant to revive us emotionally, mentally, physically, and spiritually.

Are You In Need of Rest?

God intimately knows our bodies—after all, He crafted them! He designed us not just to move, but also to rest and refuel through proper sleep, nutrition, and exercise. It's vital to remember that our bodies need time to recover from the daily grind to replenish energy and maintain strength. Neglecting rest can unravel not only our physical health but also our mental and spiritual well-being.

A poignant reminder of this is seen in the story of Elijah from 1 Kings 19. Facing threats to his life and burdened by exhaustion, Elijah was on the brink of collapse. But God didn't just urge him to push through; instead, He instructed Elijah to eat and rest. This simple act of replenishing his body and spirit empowered him to continue his journey and accomplish the monumental tasks God set before him.

So, take a cue from Elijah—don't underestimate the power of rest. Allow yourself the downtime you need to stay sharp and spirited for all that life throws your way. After all, even the most steadfast need their rest to forge ahead and do great things.

Mental and Spiritual Rest Matters

Mental and spiritual rest are crucial, yet often overlooked aspects of our well-being. Just as leaders in the Old Testament took Sabbath breaks to rest their minds, we too need mental downtime. The relentless pace of modern life can leave our brains exhausted and prone to anxiety and depression. It's essential to pause and engage in activities that allow our minds to relax, such as meditation or prayer. These practices not only refresh our mental state but connect us spiritually by opening a dialogue with God when we're overwhelmed.

Spiritual rest should be a priority, as emphasized in Psalm 27:4 where David speaks of his deep desire to dwell with God continually. In the hustle of daily responsibilities, it's often our spiritual practices that are first sacrificed.

Remember the wise words often attributed to Adrian Rogers, "If the devil can't make you bad, he'll make you busy." Or as I like to say, "Hustle is a system the enemy created for us to bless ourselves, it ain't biblical, so it's bad" LOL

Rest in Action

To begin to emphasize and prioritize rest in your life, as a woman of influence, called to impact and generate millions, evaluate the things you are "hustling" in and hand them over to God. Prioritizing moments where you are regularly stepping back to recharge and reconnect with your faith. This will help you harness the potential to expand your capabilities and influence dramatically.

Faith it Now: Embracing Divine Rest

Task: Crafting Your Sabbath Practice

This exercise is designed to help you establish a Sabbath practice that resonates with your personal and professional life, enabling you to experience the fullness of God's promise of rest.

Reflect on Your Current Rhythms:

- Spend some quiet time reflecting on your current work and rest patterns. Are you giving yourself time to fully recover and connect with God, or are you caught in a cycle of continuous labor?

Define Your Sabbath:

- What does a day of rest look like for you? Remember, Sabbath rest isn't necessarily idleness; it's about activities that restore and rejuvenate your spirit, body, and mind. Define activities that you will abstain from and activities that will help you recharge.

Plan Your Sabbath Day:

- Choose a day in the upcoming week to practice your Sabbath. Mark it on your calendar. Plan how you will spend the day—include restful activities like prayer, meditation, reading scripture, spending time in nature, or whatever helps you feel renewed.

Set Boundaries:

- Inform your family, friends, and colleagues (if necessary) about your Sabbath practice. Setting these boundaries is crucial for making your day of rest possible. This might include turning off your phone, staying away from emails, or any other work-related tasks.

Journal Your Experience:

- After your Sabbath day, take some time to journal about the experience. How did it affect your physical, mental, and spiritual well-being? What insights did you gain about God's provision and rest?

Adjust and Persist:

- Reflect on what worked and what didn't. Adjust your plans for the next Sabbath accordingly. The goal is to make this practice a consistent part of your life, allowing you to regularly tap into God's restorative power.

Commit to Continuous Practice:

Make a commitment to observe this Sabbath practice for the next four weeks. Note the changes in your stress levels, productivity, and spiritual health. Share your journey in our Facebook community using the hashtag #FaithItNowRest, and encourage others with your testimony of embracing divine rest.

CHAPTER 2:
THE CALL FOR CLARITY

"It Happened in my mind,
then I held it in my hands"
- TAUSHAUNA

There is a unique principle of faith mentioned in Mark 11:24, that states if you stand asking for anything, believe that you have them and then receive them. This principle implies that faith is a finished work, once you mentally receive what you have asked for. It's so simple that people actually over complicate it, but I totally understand how and why.

You see, faith in itself is all about your mind perceiving that what you are hoping for, anticipating, and even expecting is real, without anything actually being realized. Hebrews 11:1 says this: faith is the substance of things hoped for, the evidence of things not seen. And so faith is such a unique gift because it partners with our mind and our imagination, which in turns ignites our vision, and all of our hopes are fueled by this notion, and evidence that what we perceive is actually coming to pass.

So then how do we move from this concept, to actual, conception? Well the bible tells us that faith is only summoned by what we hear. In Romans it mentions how "So then faith comes by hearing..", so if you are going to conceive anything by faith, you must first be hearing things that are in alignment with what you intend to believe God for. Hearing is the only prerequisite for faith coming into your life. The more you hear something, the stronger your faith becomes in that area, or about that thing.

For me, it was essential that whenever God imparted a word to me, I needed to grasp it with full clarity, especially regarding my journey to a 7-figure year. As a visionary woman like you, the more I heard His word and believed it, the more vividly I could see it in my mind. I realized that if I could keep that vision alive in my thoughts long enough, it would eventually sink into my heart because, as Proverbs 23:7 suggests, what we dwell on in our minds becomes woven into our hearts, and we become that. Once that vision nested in my heart, it transformed into a genuine desire. The Bible promises that God grants the desires of our heart. Furthermore, what fills our hearts abundantly will inevitably spill out of our mouths according to Matthew 12:34, the very mouths endowed with the power to create realities (proverb 18:21)! So, I knew that if I nurtured the thought in my heart, it wouldn't be long before it manifested into something I could touch and hold!

Clarity is the Building Block of Vision

For years, I've been fueled by a deep-seated desire to amass wealth—not for personal gain, but because I've always felt called to greatness, to empower and bless others. This drive to uplift people has been a constant in my life, much like my role as a point guard in basketball, where setting up teammates to score was my calling. Yet, when the pressure was on, I never hesitated to take the crucial shot myself. This proactive spirit carried over into my journey as a full-time entrepreneur, intensifying my sense of purpose to build people and God's Kingdom.

I quickly realized that my ability to make a significant impact was directly linked to the extent of my resources. The desire for wealth, therefore, was never about affluence for its own sake but about having the means to fulfill needs. My understanding of the power of vocalizing my vision became transformative during a period when I learned the immense value of my voice. I discovered that vision is voice-activated: speaking out or decreeing something could indeed make it manifest, a concept I explored deeply in my first devotional, *Voice the Vision, Releasing God's Promises Over Your Life*.

Embracing this principle, I started to affirm my aspirations daily, particularly my goal to become a millionaire and a conduit of Kingdom wealth—a trusted steward who could distribute resources across nations, embodying the biblical ideal of being a lender, not a borrower. I repeated these affirmations and others I received in prayer until they built up my faith to the point where I could not only envision but feel the reality of these desires.

This drive became even more potent in the year I gained absolute clarity about my divine calling in the marketplace, understanding precisely what God intended for me to achieve.

The Visions that changed it all.

The day was December 17th 2022, and I was in deep prayer and meditation when God began to show me a vision of Psalm 23 playing out with me in it. He was literally walking with me in green pastures, and then on the green pastures was a money tree. I went to lay under the tree and God said to me, beyond the money I want to give you land to plant and to transform. After I agreed, many many tents begin to pop up and then God led me to the water bank, I sat at the river, put my feet in the water and then a table appeared out of the water about 5 feet away from me, everything on it was gold and it looked like a feast of food, and then it came closer to me within reach and it was the home and neighborhood we desired on it, then there was tons of other things on this table and God said you will have everything I showed you.

He proceeds to tell me things like how He is about to take me higher, and that I am about to see sudden drastic changes of increase come into my life. All good stuff right? Absolutely. However, the very next day, I was surrounded with anxiety, fear, and worry, after I got a call that shifted everything and made me forget such a glorious encounter. #Redflag

Counterfeits and Confusion Before Clarity

In just 24 hours, there was a shift and it wasn't in my favor. The feelings I felt were all the result of a burden disguised as a blessing.

I had gotten a call the next day for a job at a marketing agency, and in my mind it was in alignment with the vision and word I received. However, the feelings of fear, anxiety, and worry were, in this case, indicators that this was not from God. You see these emotions were the result of a conversation my husband had with me about the job, once we laid everything out on the table. The truth was, the job was 30 minutes away from my home, I was still nursing my 1 year old baby, , we only had 1 car, and my husband was working too, and we had no babysitter. Sheesh writing that makes me realize how much of a stretch this was.

It took my husband to point out to me that I was going to be operating from a place of toil and neglecting the 3 main important areas of rest in order to properly function as God requires.

After realizing this very real truth, I recognized that this was not the move, but indeed a counterfeit. God wouldn't send me anything that would jeopardize my rest and overall health (spiritual, mental, physical, and financial health).

In hindsight, I know this was a counterfeit blessing because my clarity was on the way. However, many times we are sidetracked by the counterfeit because it resembles a "word" or "prophecy" we received, and we ignore the signs that this is wrong, and try to make it fit what God says.

You can tell a counterfeit blessing from the real blessing, because the counterfeit will always interrupt your rest! It will interrupt or compromise your peace, mentally, spiritually, physically, or financially. So if you are in a position, circumstance or situation that strongly resembles a blessing, but your rest and peace in these areas have been compromised. Walk or run away!

God is a God of order, cleanliness, and clarity, so if there is disorder, messiness or confusion in it, it is never from Him. As a matter of fact, the bible firmly states that He is not the author of confusion. Confusion is written on the hearts and minds of people to keep them from gaining clarity around subject matters that can prosper them. It is a tool and subtle weapon of the enemy that works time and time again, robbing people of purpose, destiny, and even prosperity. However once you gain clarity, so much will follow you.

{POWER PAUSE}

Join in on the discussion usings #counterfeitmoment in our facebook group, and answer this question in the chat.

The blessing or the burden

Are you wondering if that blessing that just fell into your lap is a blessing or a burden. Remember this, If God sent it, it will not compromise your mental, spiritual, or physical health. It will align with all three, because God always wants us at our optimal best, and available for Him. What was one thing that appeared to be a blessing, but you realized it was a counterfeit, on your road to 7-figures?

A Second Touch is Okay

Not long after that, I received another vision after I decided to meditate on the word of God for more clarity around the situation.

Listen, do not be afraid to go back to God. As a matter of fact in instances of faith, being isolated and getting alone with God, and asking for more clarity is necessary. It was for the blind man, who needed a second touch in order to finally see clearly.

24

The man looked up and said, "I can see the people, but they look like trees walking around."

25

Once again Jesus placed His hands on the man's eyes, and when he opened them his sight was restored, and he could see everything clearly. (Mark 8:24-25)

So I went back to God for a second time and asked,

"God , is this you? " I am calling on you to "SHOW ME " great and mighty things that I know not Lord. I need you".

What I didn't realize is that I was unlocking a mystery and a crucial principle of faith. It was the principle of vision. Most people will only think that the principle of vision is connected to Habbakuk 2:2, when indeed, Jeremiah 33:3 is a principle of vision we can easily tap into by simply calling on God and asking Him for answers, the word states that He will show us great things.

Call to Me, and I will answer you, and show you great and 2 mighty things, which you do not know (jer. 33:3)

Moments later, I got a vision of an elite agency, with my team, my husband, real estate deals, housing contracts, branding deals, and marketing management, the whole nine yards, and it was *OURS!*

God was telling and showing me what *HE WANTED ME TO HAVE* and What was planned in my books of destiny if I stayed the course. Then He put this insatiable desire to travel and speak in my belly again. Something I always desired, and had done occasionally, but this desire felt like this was my profession. I stood in that feeling for days, until one day while I was writing He spoke plainly and gave me clarity on what I was supposed to do.

Fasting, the Breeding Ground for Clarity

One of the main prayer requests I get from women and me, is for clarity, direction, guidance. Many are seeking clarity and peace knowing their purpose, and I was in the middle of a 40 day fast when God gave me the clarity I was seeking.

Spiritual fasting, when done correctly and intentionally, will bring so much clarity and understanding to your life. Revelation is a byproduct of spiritual fasting when done correctly and intentionally. I say correctly and intentionally because many times our motives to fast, even spiritual fasting is typically result driven, rather than capacity focused. Spiritual fasting should be done to increase you. The reverence should be on God, His word, and aligning with His will in regards to what you are led to fast about. Reading your bible and prayer should not be neglected, they should actually be done during the times you would typically eat. Again, a tremendous resource for understanding fasting is a book by my old coach, and a mentor for life, Lenika Scott. She has a book called Fasting For A Breakthrough that is fantastic! You can order it directly from www.lenikascott.com. I also have a free training available on fasting in our Facebook group that you can access here: www.facebook.com/groups/7figurefaith

On this particular fast for me, in the middle of my time journaling to God, I got the clarity around my purpose and who I was called to help, in order to make that vision of the agency and all that God showed us visible.

This was huge because every vision God gives you needs a vehicle that will bring it to pass! Your purpose and the people your purpose serves is the vehicle that helps you fulfill the vision. God spoke plain and simple to me on that day, and all the dead ends in trying to discover my niche, my people, and listening to "entrepreneurial gurus" came to a halt. I was clear and at peace.

After 10 years of toiling as an entrepreneur, 4 weeks into my fast God gave me my "niche", or what I like to say, my nations!

God told me that I was called to impact the marketplace by helping kingdom moms in ministry amplify their voice and message in multiple premium media outlets! I was ecstatic. Nevermind the fact I didn't know what was next, that wasn't my business. The fact was I had a starting point. A foundation had begun.

Get Clear About Your Call

It's important to understand that until you are clear, you will unintentionally invite toil and stress, and that hustle mentality into your plight to impact millions. So be sure to activate the principle of clarity in your life.

To gain clarity, you need vision, and that vision needs to be activated with your voice, fasting, and a faith increase.

Have you called on God and asked Him to show you your heavenly blueprints? Or what's in the books of your destiny? This is a principle that is the foundation of my 7 step Framework to 7-figures, and that is CLARITY! You have to get clear on what Heaven has planned and written for you, because that work is already complete, it just needs your participation and faith to activate it!

God is a God of clarity, so confusion is never from Him. As a matter of fact, the bible firmly states that He is not the author of confusion. Confusion is written on the hearts and minds of people to keep them from gaining clarity around subject matters that can prosper them. It is a tool and subtle weapon of the enemy that works time and time again, robbing people of purpose, destiny, and even prosperity. However once you gain clarity, so much will follow you.

Faith it Now: Embracing Clarity

The Power of Clarity

Clarity is not just a tool; it's a weapon for those destined to win. It not only sets the stage for financial achievements—whether that's reaching 6, 7, or even 8-figure incomes—but also fosters growth and expansion. Let's explore how clarity can transform your environment:

- ***Peace:***

  Clear vision removes uncertainty, fear, and doubt, enriching trust and boosting confidence among all involved. This serenity is invaluable as it anchors your endeavors and soothes the spirit.

- ***Confidence:***

  With clarity comes stability. Knowing your direction allows for structured growth and informed risk-taking, reducing penalties for mistakes because goals are well understood.

- ***Passion and Purpose:***

  Understanding your clear path enhances your drive and aligns your actions with your true purpose, unlocking your full potential and affirming your identity.

- ***Value:***

Clarity enriches your spiritual, emotional, and mental well-being, enhancing how you value yourself and your mission.

- ***Impact:***

Clear objectives lead to measurable impacts personally, relationally, and financially, paving the way for broader influence and deeper connections.

Faith It Now Exercise:

This week, take a moment to seek solitude and clarity:

- ***Ask God:*** "Where would you like to bring clarity in my life? In my business? Show me great and mighty things I do not know."
- Consider embarking on a spiritual fast to deepen this inquiry, focusing on areas of your life that impact your faith.

Community Sharing:

Share your insights and experiences in our Facebook group using the hashtag #7FigureClarity. Join the conversation and get a chance to win in our $1k monthly giveaways for active participants or our annual $1k drawing for members who post a book review.

Join the Journey:

Your path to clarity is a shared journey. Post your clarity breakthroughs and witness how transparency and clear vision can transform not just your business, but every aspect of your life. Welcome to a world where clarity paves the way to success!

CHAPTER 3:

OPTIMIZING YOUR OPPORTUNITIES

The Opportunity to Obey

Clarity brings a unique responsibility to seize opportunities and to boldly *GO FORTH* and Occupy the territory that is now laid out for you. Well atleast, that's what I have come to learn. The moment I gained clarity on my assignment my instructions were to GO! It was as if the urgency of that word had kicked in and the vehicle that was carrying the vision was a rocketship and it was nearly time for me to launch. Will you accept or deny what is presented? It's your decision.

I learned a very powerful lesson on the backend of clarity. Not only does clarity create a clear path to destiny, but clarity, when presented, will offer you the opportunity to make a decision.That decision, that many refer to as "giving God your yes" or a simple acceptance of the call presented, is often followed up with instructions to obey. How you obey those instructions will either lead you on a path of destiny or delay.

Please know and understand destiny always requires a decision. And that decision will require more decisions that will continue to align you with your destiny until the final destination is reached. If you're reading this book your next destination is 7 figures. Whether that is your final destination depends on the decisions you make, and the vision connected to God's purpose and potential for your life. Nonetheless, I can promise you that when you make the right decisions, in alignment with your destiny, doors of opportunity will present themselves for you. Your responsibility in those moments are to do these three things:

1. ***Obey the instructions or strategy that you are given in its entirety***
2. ***Execute those instructions with excellence***
3. ***Occupy with persistence***

The Principle of Obedience

I've always heard that obedience opens doors, and I know that to be a fact. However, I also learned that obedience does a lot more than open doors, it closes them as well. Obedience aligns you with your destiny, and therefore not only adds the right things and opportunities to your life, but it also will remove the wrong things or the things that no longer serve this version of yourself.

Obedience requires discipline and respect to the goal or task at hand. It shows that you are ready, willing and capable of following instruction and that you value the wishes of the person, group, or in the case of destiny, that you value the plans and voice of God and you are willing to please Him.

If you are going to operate in faith, especially 7-figure faith, obedience is a requirement. However, obedience does not require faith in the same way that faith requires obedience. For example, when you are on your job, working your 20, 40 or even 80 hours, you are obedient to the schedule your boss gave you. You revere and respect the schedule, but only because the results are already revealed. It requires absolutely no faith on your part, to believe that your check will come every two weeks, month, or whatever your pay cycle. No faith, just loyalty to the routine. As long as you are obedient to the routine then, you will receive.

In one of my favorite books in the bible, Deuteronomy, specifically chapter 28, God speaks of the blessings of obedience. However, not just obedience of any kind, it is the obedience to keeping His instructions. It reads:

If you fully obey the Lord your God and carefully keep all his commands that I am giving you today, the Lord your God will set you high above all the nations of the world.

2

You will experience all these blessings if you obey the Lord your God:

3

Your towns and your fields will be blessed.

4

Your children and your crops will be blessed.
The offspring of your herds and flocks will be blessed.

5

Your fruit baskets and breadboards will be blessed.

6

Wherever you go and whatever you do, you will be blessed.

7

"The Lord will conquer your enemies when they attack you. They will attack you from one direction, but they will scatter from you in seven!

8

"The Lord will guarantee a blessing on everything you do and will fill your storehouses with grain. The Lord your God will bless you in the land he is giving you.

9

"If you obey the commands of the Lord your God and walk in his ways, the Lord will establish you as his holy people as he swore he would do.

10

Then all the nations of the world will see that you are a people claimed by the Lord, and they will stand in awe of you.

11

"The Lord will give you prosperity in the land he swore to your ancestors to give you, blessing you with many children, numerous livestock, and abundant crops.

12

The Lord will send rain at the proper time from his rich treasury in the heavens and will bless all the work you do. You will lend to many nations, but you will never need to borrow from them.

13

If you listen to these commands of the Lord your God that I am giving you today, and if you carefully obey them, the Lord will make you the head and not the tail, and you will always be on top and never at the bottom.

14

You must not turn away from any of the commands I am giving you today, nor follow after other gods and worship them.

This passage of scripture explains the rewards of obedience in its entirety, as it pertains to obeying God's commands or instructions. It takes great faith in the promises of what is being revealed here in order to keep and do these things that are asked.

So you may be wondering, well what was He asking of me. That is the question that your clarity call will answer.

When you, by faith and expectancy, are obedient to what was told of you, and the instructions God releases to you, it positions you and aligns you for immeasurable impact.

The Principles of Execution and Advancement:

By now, we understand how clarity brings vision, and vision when activated by faith will present the opportunity to obey God's instruction. Well in order for faith to really move and work on our behalf we have to do our part. Obedience is a verb. It doesn't just require action in order to work on your behalf, it is action. So once you receive your instructions, you must be ready and willing to G.O. aka get up and obey!

God not only wants your 7-figure faith to partner with obedience, but He wants to advance you in your faith and your destiny by giving you instruction that you can execute in order to help you GO and accomplish the vision connected to your faith!

GO FORTH!

Habbakuk 2:2-3 is where the principle of execution lies according to an in depth teaching from Dr. Cindy Trimm. In this teaching she lays out the principle of execution, referencing that the vision that God gives you, that you must vehemently obey, must not only be written, but also written plain enough for someone/you to run with the vision.

This is why it is so important that you are clear on what your 7-figure vision is. Have you written it? What's your story behind the vision? 7-figures can't merely just be a goal, but it has to become a vision that you can plainly see, and write. Once it's written it's time to execute it in order to advance and take ownership of the territory connected to the vision. Yes, the vision has territory, but unless you can execute the instructions and plans connected to bringing your vision to life, you will not fully possess or occupy the territory connected to your millions.

So have you written your vision in great detail? Have you stopped to evaluate how the things you are doing now brings you closer to the overall vision and plan connected to your millions? Are you in the right market? Does your story and brand story align? When was the last time you updated your brand strategy? These are all things that we must consider in our pursuit to elevate our faith and possess the millions we are called to impact, acquire, and distribute.

Faith it Now: Occupying Opportunities with Persistence

Embrace your mantle as a millionaire and claim your rightful territory, the domain Heaven has crafted just for you. Recognize that this isn't merely a fight for financial gain but a battle to reclaim what the enemy has unlawfully occupied. Here's how you can optimize and occupy your opportunities:

- ***Acknowledge Your Space:***

  Understand that there is a specific industry or sphere of influence that is uniquely yours. Get consumed with the idea that there's a place with your name on it—your mountain to claim.

- ***Embrace Your Identity:***

  Knowing and embracing who you are is crucial. Failing to do so can cost you spiritually and keep you from recognizing what you are entitled to.

- ***Clarify and Execute the Vision:***

  Inspired by Habakkuk 2:2, "Write the vision and make it plain on tablets, so he may run who reads it." This is about more than understanding your vision—it's about executing it with precision. Execution ignites urgency and propels you forward.

❧ ***Focus and Accountability:***

Once you're clear on your vision, optimization involves focusing intently and holding yourself accountable. Execution brings your vision to life, fostering a continuous cycle of learning and advancement.

❧ ***Seize and Occupy:***

When opportunities arise, it's crucial to act decisively. Use the strategy provided to maximize these moments. Execution and seizing opportunities are not just about embracing growth—they're about occupying the space ordained for you.

Action Step:

This week, dedicate time to identify the "territory" meant for you. Write down the vision of where you see yourself in this space, make it clear and actionable. Reflect on this vision daily and commit to taking one step towards occupying this space each day.

Join the Community:

Share your journey of seizing opportunities and executing your vision in our Facebook group. Use the hashtag #Faith2Occupy to connect with others who are also moving towards their millionaire mantle. Engage actively and you could be part of our monthly $1k giveaway for vibrant participants or our annual drawing!

Let's move forward with clarity and purpose, executing our visions and occupying our territories

CHAPTER 4:

MASTERING POTENTIAL

Can I encourage you for a moment? I just really feel the urge to remind you that what tried to kill you or take you out, that thing you survived...is about to witness you win! May I take a few more lines in this book to encourage you and remind you that where you are now, is exactly where you are supposed to be, and everything that the enemy used to deny and impede your progress, was the very thing God is using to propel you into your destiny. That pain is just fuel to increase your capacity and a measure of your potential. Here is your friendly reminder that:

You are enough. You deserve to have it. You have what it takes. You will be the first. You can start now. *YOU HAVE EVERYTHING YOU NEED TO BE SUCCESSFUL RIGHT NOW*. All of your obstacles are moving out of the way, and everything you need is on its way to you. Don't quit. Just

Release it! You have the oil for this! You are anointed for this! You have all you need!

The Importance of Potential

The third principle of our 7-Figure Faith COMPASS© is all about mastering your potential through the power of your story. I truly believe that sometimes we focus too much on one purpose, rather than our potential. When I realized that God was more concerned about me reaching and maximizing my potential rather than just figuring out my purpose. It was a game changer. The reality is, potential, when maximized, will attract purpose. Potential attracts the plans and purposes of God. How you use what's in your hands will bring the purpose that needs what's in your hands to operate.

To prove this point, I began to study parables like the 10 talents, the 5 virgins, the laborers, and the woman who fed the prophet, and realized that in all of these stories, the potential of the person was what was important. In all of these stories, they did not go out looking for purpose, instead they used what they had, multiplied it, managed it, and maintained it, and the people that needed what they had, came to them, or they reaped a reward for doing so.

When I began to understand mastering my potential, through study and always making use of what was in my possession by finding ways to increase it; I was able to fulfill more plans for God. Ultimately the plans and unlimited purposeful missions God had for me would always fit into the larger purpose and God's ultimate unfolding plan for my life, all because of my potential being maximized in that season of my life.

Potential, Purpose and Capacity

Purpose is absolutely important, it's a part of the vision and plans of God for your life, however, purpose needs potential to run efficiently and potential needs capacity in order to be maximized.

One of my all-time favorite stories in the Bible is about the widow and the oil. I actually just taught a bible lesson on this that you can watch here; https://fb.watch/rpxX5iA5sP/

Nonetheless, here are the cliff notes.

It's a tale that hits close to home for anyone who's faced seemingly insurmountable challenges. This widow wasn't just coping with her husband's loss; she was staring down a debt so severe it threatened to take her children away. As a mama bear myself—fun, loving, and the nicest person you could meet—threaten my kids, and PEACHY comes out, not just Peach!

{Power Pause: R.I.P. to the old me LOL! So glad Peachy is gone, she used to lay hands, but not the Godly ones LOL! Ok friend, back to the book.}

The Widow Woman

The story, told in 2 Kings 4:1-7, reveals a deeper lesson beyond the widow's immediate financial crisis. She seeks help from the Prophet, who instead of giving her money, challenges her to recognize her own capacity for solving problems. He asks,

"What do you want me to do for you? What do you have in your house?" This isn't dismissive but a prompt for her to utilize what she already possesses—her little bit of oil, which she underestimates at first.

She might have thought, "What can I do with this tiny bit of oil?" But following the Prophet's instructions, she gathers empty jars from her neighbors. Each jar she fills with oil, multiplying her resources, and she not only clears her debts but also secures her family's future. This story isn't just a turnaround; it's a revelation about the remnants of grace we hold—the anointing that remains no matter our losses.

Your Message and Your Potential

So, about the message this widow conveyed—she had to be something of a leader, right? She didn't just passively accept the Prophet's command. She mobilized, going door to door, her sons alongside, persuading her neighbors to lend their jars. That required trust, guts, and some persuasive communication. She wasn't asking for a small favor; she was orchestrating a comeback, gathering the resources to turn her little bit of oil into a substantial blessing.

This is a powerful reminder of how crucial our ability to communicate is. Whether it's going door to door with a plan or standing on a stage sharing our vision, how we express our challenges and solutions can open doors and create opportunities not just for us but for everyone we touch. Mastering your potential is as much about mastering your message as it is about tapping into your inner strengths.

Faith it Now: End-of-Chapter Action Task

Let's bring this home with a "Faith It Now" task that'll help you refine your message and start leveraging it effectively:

Task: Craft Your Power Message

Reflect on a significant challenge you've overcome or a unique strength you possess. Using the following structure, create a concise, powerful message:

- ***The Challenge:***

  What was the obstacle or difficulty you faced?

- ***The Victory:***

  How did you overcome it? What principles or steps were crucial?

- ***The Transformation:***

  What was the outcome? How did things change for the better?

- ***The Offer:***

  How can your story benefit or inspire others? What's the key takeaway?

First, rehearse this story by yourself, get comfortable with the flow. Then share it with a friend or mentor, gathering feedback on its clarity, impact, and emotional resonance. Refine it based on this feedback, making your story not just heard, but felt.

By crafting and sharing your message, you affirm your own journey and extend an invitation to others to embark on theirs. This isn't just storytelling; it's a launchpad for miracles, much like the widow's small jar of oil.

Share any component of your story by using the hashtag. For example to share your offer to our 7-Figure Faith'ers Facebook Community, you would share with hashtag #myoffer

CHAPTER 5:
ACTIVATION, AVAILABILITY, AND YOUR YES

I can remember being 4 years old sitting on the front row of Zion Baptist Church with my Aunt Carrie, who would take me to church with her whenever I stayed with while growing up and listening to the choir sing these words:

You gave me my hands to reach out to man
To show him Your love and Your perfect plan
You gave me my ears, I can hear Your voice so clear
I can hear the cries of sinners
But can I wipe away their tears?
You gave me my voice to speak Your Word
To sing all Your praises to those who never heard
But with my eyes I see a need for more availability
I've seen the hearts that have been broken
So many people to be free

Lord, I'm available to You
My will I give to You
I'll do what You say do
Use me Lord to show someone the way and
enable me to say
My storage is empty and I am available to You

These words have meant more to me in the last 3 years of my journey in KINGDOM entrepreneurship and one who carries an apostolic office in the marketplace, than they ever had.

As I write this, I can hear that tune in my heart and I am literally in a posture of gratitude, because even as I am encouraging and educating you on how to tap into the faith for what God has promised you, I am making my hands available for the master's use. I am recognizing my own availability at this very moment, and I am so honored to serve God and you in this moment.

I am instantly transformed to my 4 year old self as I write this, as I make the declaration to my Father to *USE ME LORD, I'M AVAILABLE.*

In this moment I want to remind you that God trusts you with the wealth and the millions of people your life, business, and ministry will impact. God is so proud of you in this moment, because whether you recognize it or not you are actively in pursuit, and this is counted unto you as *a seek* and availability. The bible reminds us that He is a rewarder of those that diligently seek Him according to Hebrews 11:6. So congrats. He sees you *seeking*.

{POWER PAUSE}

Prophetic move to pray!

I literally have to pause here, and encourage you to do the same. I was not going to add this part to the book, and I was literally about to stop typing to get on my knees and worship God. Then I heard God say, invite them into this moment with you, they need to remember what I brought them through and why I chose them to be my hands and feet for such a time as this!

He said, it wasn't because you were the most capable, or that you had any extraordinary abilities, but it was because you have made yourself AVAILABLE for the MASTER's use.

Take about 10 minutes or more to open yourself up to the power of God through worship and gratitude. If you feel an overwhelming urge to repent for delayed obedience, do so as well.

God is truly moving on me this moment, and some of you reading this I can literally feel, and feel the anointing right where you are. He is with you and regardless of what has happened or is happening He wants you to know He loves you and HE HAS NOT LOST CONFIDENCE IN YOU!

YOU WILL NOT FAIL! YOU WILL SUCCEED! GOD IS GOING TO MAKE YOU PROOF THAT WHAT HE SPOKE OVER YOUR LIFE IS MORE REAL THAN THE CIRCUMSTANCES THAT TRIED TO TAKE YOUR LIFE!

Deliverance is Happening Now

I Literally feel a strong heat on my right arm, this is a sign God gives me when He is delivering. I also feel a weight and heaviness on my shoulders, to represent burdens and stress. So whoever you are reading this, I believe deliverance just hit your house. God is delivering you and delivering it from you at this moment. My God! Raise your hands in acceptance.

If this is not you, please make yourself available and partner with the words on these pages and pray for the person that is reading and I am feeling this for.

A Prayer for Deliverance

Father in the name of Jesus, I thank you for interrupting my will in completing this chapter, in exchange for your will to complete and finish something in the life of this person. Father, I pray that your peace and power overtake them right now! I pray that every hindrance that is stopping them from being fully available and of use to you is removed.

We break ties with the hindrances that are impeding progress and advancement. We break covenant with the spirit of fear and inadequacy. God I pray that they resist the spirit of lack, that would point them towards not having everything they need to pursue your plans to increase them.

Father, increase their desire to GO FORTH and BECOME! I speak to the very thing that is hidden and has created turmoil, blockages, that has been preventing total breakthrough! By the delegated authority of Christ, I call that thing to come up and out of their life never to return.

BE FREE NOW in the name of Jesus!

In Jesus Name, Amen.

God bless you.

Ok, now that God has truly had his way, I hope you can see how serious He is about you and this season in activating your 7-figure faith. I think we are free to proceed.

Back to Your Regularly Scheduled Chapter

Recently I was in a meeting with a few multi-millionaires who were sharing their stories and their passion around making God their CEO in their business and how there is no real separation between Kingdom and your call to your industry, your industry is a part of the call on your life for Kingdom advancement. This is a concept I was all too familiar with.

While in the room, I was under the impression that I was only there to be praying for the host, a destiny partner of mine. However, God had told me earlier that day that I was supposed to be there to receive, but instead I was too busy serving to remember. Like many of us, I was so caught up in serving, because after all it's the right thing to do. However, it can become the wrong thing to do if it is making you unavailable to receive.

> *(That's a word all in itself, but I don't have enough time to take you down a rabbit hole with me, we already had deliverance service :-) If I keep this up, this book will become another one of the lost scrolls)*

So while on post, praying and being overly busy, like Martha, the speaker said something that sparked my attention because it spoke to a concept in my COMPASS framework on the *Principle of Availability.*

A Destiny Interruption

The speaker who caught my attention and is ultimately responsible for the urge to even get this book completed was Kingdom CEO, Jaylen LaGrande, the founder of the 316 collection. He was a perfectly placed person in a season where God was requiring me to go higher.

He begin to speak on Isaiah 55:11 that says:

> *So shall my word be that goeth forth out of my mouth: it shall not return unto me void, but it shall accomplish that which I please, and it shall prosper in the thing whereto I sent it.*

However, the revelation and the approach He took to a familiar text, challenged us all in the room, not to take ownership of the word or prophetic instruction God gives us, but to take accountability for the word He spoke, by taking action and making yourself available to carry it out. Jaylen said that God's word, which cannot return unto Him void, essentially is released in the hearts and minds of His children as ideas and plans for Him to partner with them and accomplish. However, the problem that happens with most people is that they are more focused on their ability rather than their availability.

So when their million dollar moment comes to them in the form of an idea, task, or assignment, many will let the moment pass because they are paralyzed by the fear or inadequacy of their lack of time, money, or resources, aka their ability. Rather than move, they stand still and miss the moment.

Meanwhile, that word that God spoke, or assignment, still has to accomplish what God sent it out to do; it is hovering over the Earth looking for someone who is more focused on being available rather than their abilities. It will accomplish what it set out to do, with or without you.

Don't' Miss your Moment

As a person with 7-figure faith, we must not fall into this trap or the carnal thinking of "What God has for me is for me", while that is true, the unspoken reality is, what God has for you is for you unless you reject it. This is why many who don't move on the commission to pursue a million dollar idea, the global assignment, or divine collaboration, will witness someone do the very thing that God told them to do, and be upset or feel like they missed out. Their lack of availability, cost them the window and grace to pursue the opportunity. They still may do the thing God asked of them, but the grace to do it with ease may have passed, or it may take them longer to accomplish than it would have if they would have moved when God said so.

Grace Does Abound

The year God called my husband and I into ministry together was actually in 2013. I remember writing the plans up for our ministry, ideas, and the "Soul'd Out" Summer bible studies and prayers, city wide baptisms we were going to host, the whole nine. I remember going to get permission from our leaders and feeling rejected when nothing was approved. That rejection hit me hard, but it also impacted us in a way that we slowly made ourselves unavailable in the way God intended to use us. We served, but it was serving while busy, instead of advancing the Kingdom in the way we were created to.

After 10 years of serving, the call to do ministry together officially presented itself in a mighty way. We had always done ministry and supported each other, my husband would minister in the church and in the pulpit, and I would minister in the marketplace and online. We supported each other heavily, and he was so proud of me, but those were our worlds, we didn't think they meshed lol. I literally would tremble to preach in a pulpit, and my husband most certainly couldn't fathom "preaching to people who aren't there" LOL And now we have a global ministry that is based online, with prayer hubs across the nation.

Our ministry LNB International Ministries is a global platform that empowers people no matter where they are in the world both in and outside of the church. We are truly a church without walls.

The Call to Availability

God commissioned and sent us to Florida in 2021. We were only given the instructions to plant, and be planted until He moves us. We knew we were to build and start a ministry, but we didn't know what that was supposed to look like. We made the move, and immediately became unavailable to the way God intended to use us, until March of 2023. During our first years we tried to figure everything out, and do things only according to our ability, personal cash flow, and personal strengths. You want to get God upset. Put yourself in delay, and watch Him get your attention.

{POWER PAUSE}

7 Figure Faith, and any form of faith for that matter does not need your help in figuring out anything. As a matter of fact, faith and figuring it out cannot coexist. Furthermore, God doesn't give us a commission or call, and expects us to have to figure it out. He just wants us to trust Him enough to let Him use us according to His will and His plans.

As we began to do the regular things, like find a church, a pastor, and get busy with the ministry, we still were unfulfilled. These were all things that satisfied our comfort zones, but not our true commission. Our actual commission to go had more to do with the principle of availability, which is giving God a complete yes in faith and trust. Being truly ready for the Master's use, no matter the cost, or how uncomfortable it makes you feel.

This is the nature of every call, commission, and assignment, including your assignment to millions. It will cost you comfort, and require you to give a complete yes. You will forgo your choice on how, when, where, and even with whom, you can exercise the gift, assignment, or call to. This is what people with big faith, 7-figure faith, understand. The assignment is not yours, so you don't get to choose the "how to's" of the matter, just a yes in it's totally is all that matters.

A Complete Yes

Many have learned the hard way or come to know that when we are assigned to a God-sized mission, we must give God permission to do exactly what He wants and how He wants within our current abilities without limitations on our availability. It is a full surrender of how things need to work, and a complete submission to what your yes has afforded you.

A complete yes, takes faith, trust, and blind obedience. However, when you make yourself available in totality, the benefits come in warped speed.

Everything for you is accelerated, and restoration becomes a true reality.

I can recall going back to God one day after a robust service with our members of the LNB community. Up until that point we had been coming together for 200 days consecutively, and had just come back from our prayer retreat, when I began to reflect on the impact of our complete yes to God. The impact we were able to witness, the miracles, the total transformation, and the altars that were raised to Christ, from a single act of obedience, had me in uncontrollably tears of gratitude. I begin to thank God for allowing grace to come back and get us, and for His mercy allowing us to operate and partner with Him within this assignment.

A somber feeling came over me, as I asked God, what it would have cost us if we had not come into complete alignment with His will for our ministry. I asked, Lord, what if we would have stayed in a place of comfort, and continued to limit ourselves to the opinion of men, and our own limited perspective of who we are. What if our yes to you was limited?

His response : "A partial yes, is a whole no." God told me, it would have cost us another 10 years of waiting and frustration. He said you wouldn't have survived. You would have been heavily depressed because you would have felt like a window shopper of my glory. Knowing you were called to more, but not being able to access it.

This response should be an eye opener and added incentive for you on your road to 7-figure faith and the impact you are called to carry. Do not let anything limit your yes and complete submission to God through availing yourself to His assignment and call on your life.

Faith it Now:
The Power Principle: YES

We truly have no idea the power and the vastness of what God can do for us and through us when we are available. Your yes--- your availability over your abilities--- will magnify the power and presence of God in your business, industry, life and family. Through activating your yes, you step into a realm of faith that makes your mission to impact millions a reality. Embrace this power principle and watch the divine power, favor, and will of God align you with everything connected to your destiny, and empower you to fully function in 7-figure faith.

The Components of Your Yes:

1. Yielding: this requires us to intentionally let go of our own personal plans, limiting self-beliefs, and submitting to the will of God regardless of our personal abilities, and completely make ourselves available
2. Expectation: the truest form of faith, and the breeding ground for the miraculous. Initiating expectancy through faith will position God to truly blow your mind and move through you without restrictions.

3. Submission: this is a daily commitment to trust and align with the plans and the will of God for completion of the work, assignment, or call.

Activate Your Yes:

This week, take some intentional alone time with God to activate and re-comment your YES.

1. Initiate and Assess: Ask God what did your yes afford you, and what would it have cost you, if you didn't fully submit or activate your complete yes. If you find that you are in a position where you are partially committed to the call on your life, be it, not fully living up to your potential or doing God's thing, your way;
2. Commit and Reconnect: make a decision that this mission to millions is deserving of a complete Yes. Make a list of anything that could be standing in your way to fully submit. Evaluate this list and commit to fully submitting .
3. Repent and Go Forth: Review your list and repent for delayed obedience, and resistance in these areas. Let God move in your heart and then boldly embrace your newly revived journey. Go forth in faith and impact!

Record what God gives you in a journal, and share your gratitude and how your Yes to God has impacted your life, family, business and ministry. Use #YesActivated when you share in our community.

CHAPTER 6:
PRAYER AND THE POWER OF A.S.K.ING!

This is absolutely my favorite and the most powerful weapon you have in walking right into your mantle for millions and increasing to 7-Figure Faith. Prayer, all matters of prayer, are your invitation for the supernatural power, insight, strategy, and will of God to infuse your journey. Prayer is not only your direct line of communication with God, and a legal procedure granting God access to move on your behalf.

The importance and power of prayer in the life of the believer is one of the most underrated and also widely misused tactics of spiritual growth and expansion. Prayer is a sovereign tool that God uses to initiate dominance through the believer and delegate authority. In your prayers, you are able to see, hear, be present and even speak in the supernatural realm.

Also, prayer is the one weapon that enables us to gain a trusted and authentic relationship with God. It strengthens our trust in God and consistency in prayer fortifieds our commitment to God and He rewards us for it. (Remember, He is a rewarder of those who diligently seek Him)

I have always had a desire to pray, and intercede for others, and honestly would always be in prayer, but when it came time for me to exercise my 7 figure faith, God called me to elevate my prayer life. This elevation involved not just extending my prayer times but transforming my heart's posture. It required me to refine the intention, sacredness, diversity, and appreciation of my prayer life as I prepared for the influx of millions.

The Importance of Prayer for your 7-Figure Faith

I can easily get caught up and teach 50/11 perspectives of prayer on this topic, but in a moment of divine clarity, as I sought God's direction for what He wanted you to understand about prayer, in this chapter, I felt a sweet, gentle presence. And He impressed upon me the necessity of teaching you the power of Your "Ask" in this season.

He said "I want them to ASK".

I want them to understand the power I have granted them in ASKING, and the unlocking that unfolds in the process of A.S.K.ing according to Matthew 7:7,"Ask and it will be given to you; seek and you will find; knock and the door will be opened to you

The Power of Asking in Prayer

Can I submit to you that, after 6 chapters into this book, you are not the AVERAGE person. You have a prayer life, you understand the power of prayer, You seek God for guidance and even want to be rightly aligned with Him in all aspects of your life. I know this because He wouldn't trust you with millions, if you didn't know at this moment, I want you to know that God wants you to be okay with ASKING, for what you want. You have mastered asking for everyone else, but it's your time now. He said you have qualified for the EXCEEDINGLY and ABUNDANTLY of what is connected to what you desire.

Your access is connected to your posture in your season of asking. Don't be afraid to ask. As a matter of fact, it is through our asking, that God will be able to present the proper doors to secure the millions connected to our impact, influence and income.

The Three Components of ASKing

Let's discuss the strategy of the A.S.K. as a prayer. The "Ask" is an audacious process of prayer that isn't prideful but patient. It has 3 components which are crucial to making your prayers truly visible and a reality for you.

The Principle of ASKING

This is the most important part, it is a detailed request of what you truly desire from God. This desire based prayer is not a selfish one, but rather a supernatural one, because you are vocally requesting that God do what He said in Psalm 37:4, in that He will give you the desires of your heart, in the event you have delighted yourself in Him. These desires are the things, the ideas, the wants that keep you up at night. They are layered with your passion and connected to God's will and purpose for your life. This "Asking" prayer then acts as an igniter for the manifestation of those desires you harvest from your heart.

- Asking aligns you with God's plan and promises, and the bonuses' of Heaven that God said are a part of your *daily benefits* package (Psalms 68:19-21). There are so many things you have not received because you neglected to simply Ask.

Asking God paves the way to asking man, much like Jesus who grew in wisdom and stature, gaining favor both with God and man (Luke 2:52). This divine blueprint shows us that when we are aligned with God, we can approach our earthly interactions with the same confidence. This assurance translates directly into our business practices—from requesting a sale to sealing a deal, from pursuing a promotion to seizing new opportunities. Being in the room with the power to make these ask's is not by chance; it's by divine appointment.

When you've petitioned your Heavenly Father, you've already received the green light in the spiritual realm, granting you the boldness to make those same requests on Earth. This is the essence of active faith, bridging the gap between divine approval and earthly action. Remember, people aren't mind readers, empowered by divine insight to anticipate our needs. While we might occasionally experience serendipitous acts of kindness, the journey to a seven-figure faith typically involves making our needs and desires explicitly known.

This isn't just wishful thinking; it's faith put into action, a fundamental step towards achieving our God-given potential and prosperity. Embrace the model Jesus set, actively seeking favor with God and man as you walk confidently in your calling.

The Principle of the SEEK

The second component of asking is *the seek*. It's actually the moment in prayer where mediation is required. This is an inward seek, for the answers and solutions of our asking. When you are called to seek, it's a profound moment of listening—a time to intentionally absorb and prepare to act on what is revealed to you.

As you listen, God's responses generally fall into three categories, each demanding a specific type of obedience:

1. ***Be Still***: Sometimes, God's message is one of patience. He may instruct you to hold steady, indicating a season of waiting. This is not a passive time but one of active preparation and reflection, tuning in closely to God's timing and will.
2. ***Warning***: At other times, God may issue a caution—a clear signal to stop, step back, repent, or abandon a planned path. This response is crucial to avoid potential pitfalls and align closer with His divine wisdom.

3. ***Pursue:*** Lastly, you might receive a directive to move forward. This is a call to action, to pursue, advance, or seize opportunities laid out for you. God's command to go is an empowering prompt to engage actively with your faith and His plans for you.

In every instance, whether called to pause, halt, or proceed, your ultimate response must be one of complete obedience. This alignment ensures that you are moving in harmony with God's purpose, ready to respond aptly to His divine guidance in your life.

Types of Answers we Get	***The Actions God wants***
Be Still	God wants you to Wait
Warning	God wants you to Stop
Pursue	God wants you to Go

Whatever you get in your seek, be sure to take action, because the action you take after that will align you with God's will for your life and ultimately present doors of opportunities for you.

The Principle of KNOCKING

Knocking isn't just about opening a door; it's a principle of activation. It symbolizes your readiness to step into a new season. and embrace the growth, elevation, and renewal—what I like to call the new wineskin—that awaits. As you transition from seeking to knocking, old mindsets that no longer serve the millionaire version of you will be shed. This transition is your coronation phase, preparing you to be announced when new doors of opportunity swing open.

Deepen Your Prayer Life

In this season of elevated faith, sincerity in your prayer process is key. Be specific with God; He's ready to fulfill your requests and exceed your expectations. Don't hesitate to activate your ask—there's no wrong way to communicate your needs and desires. Just ask.

Faith it Now: Maximize Your A.S.K.ing

To truly activate the principles discussed in this chapter and cultivate a dynamic and powerful prayer life, engage in these transformative practices. Each step is designed to deepen your connection with God and reinforce your pathway to significant spiritual and worldly achievements.

Create a Dedicated Prayer Space

- Action Step: Identify a quiet corner or specific room in your home that you can dedicate to prayer and meditation. Decorate it with items that inspire serenity and devotion—perhaps candles, a Bible, inspirational writings, or simple decor that speaks to peace and reflection.

Set Regular Appointments with God

- Action Step: Schedule daily prayer time as you would any crucial appointment. Whether it's first thing in the morning, during a lunch break, or in the evening, make this non-negotiable time a cornerstone of your day.

Offer the First Fruits of Your Day

- ❧ Action Step: Start each day by dedicating your first thoughts and expressions to God. This could be a simple prayer of gratitude, a scripture reading, or a meditative moment to set the tone for the day.

Consult God in All Decisions

- ❧ Action Step: Before making any significant decision, whether personal or professional, take a moment to pray for guidance. This practice ensures that God's wisdom is at the forefront of your choices, influencing outcomes positively.

Embrace Spiritual Fasting

- ❧ Action Step: Commit to a regular fasting schedule that suits your health and spiritual needs. Begin with one day a month and consider gradually increasing as you feel led. Use this time to abstain from distractions and focus deeply on your spiritual goals and requests.

Implementing these steps will not only strengthen your relationship with God but also empower you to boldly make your requests known, both in heaven and on earth. This is your active faith in action—prepare to see doors open and your path clear as you align more closely with God's vision for your life.

CHAPTER 7:

SURRENDERING: THE 6 FIGURE SURRENDER

"Lord, I'm done. I can't do this anymore."

"I think I'll just get a job. This is too much."

"I'm tired of helping everyone else, and no one has the capacity to help me."

"The strategies you give me work for everyone else BUT me. I feel like a fraud, and I'm over it. I think I'll just go back to sales."

These were the words I found myself saying as I sat at my computer, staring at yet another bank alert warning that my account had dipped below the $50 mark. I was overwhelmed with frustration, unable to pinpoint whom I was supposed to serve as a coach or speaker, or even what my place was in the marketplace anymore. I was too talented, good at too many things, and pathless.

Can you relate? Have you been here?

Throwing money at various ventures, and investment strategies, HOPING, one would stick. Telling yourself you are creating multiple streams of income, when in reality, it's becoming multiple wells of dried up wishes and wants.

It's ok, I know that place all too well. Holding on to a word and prophecy that you have been pregnant with for years, but wondering when it was going to be time to PUSH!

The Principle of Surrender

I learned alot about this moment after studying many other Kingdom millionaires and billionaires, and I recognized a pattern. So many people that were truly successful as Kingdom business owners, ministry leaders, christian professionals, and just kingdom leaders in general, all came to a crossroad of surrendering their plans, to embrace God's will.

In hindsight I realize that surrendering isn't a pattern, but it was a principle of allowing God to take total control. People surrender in many different ways, some have to hit rock bottom after trying all 50/11 of their own plans, like me. Others, just naturally wave the white flag after seeing what not surrendering cost other people.

No matter how you surrender, it is a necessary part of your process to impact and generate millions. I discovered this was true for some of my personal mentors and even mentors from afar. People like Myron Golden, Miles Munroe, Cindy Trimm, Sonya and Dwayne Mickens, Priscilla Shirer, Damon

Dilliard, Lenika Scott, Dr. Kynan Bridges, Tabitha Russell, Jewel Tankard, Robert Tisdale, Avery Burrel Jr., and countless other great leaders of faith I would learn and glean from, all spoke of the moment they had to surrender their personal plans and agenda, to the plans and will of God, in order to truly walk and live in their purpose.and impact on the level they are called to. This was the price they paid for God to truly get the glory out of their lives.

Now it was my turn.

What Does Surrender Look Like?

Surrendering is a heart posture. It is a sincere place of submission and being okay with not knowing what's next, as long as the presence of God doesn't leave your life. It's the excitement of knowing that you don't care about the credit for anything that happens in your life, so long as God gets the glory.

In war, surrendering looks like waving a white flag of defeat, in hopes that your opponent shows mercy on you, and stops their pursuit. However, in the Kingdom, surrendering is waving a white flag of victory in hopes that God extends even more grace to you, in hopes that you can partner with His will and Heaven's blueprint for your life.

And that's where I was. On the battlefield exhausted from trying to do a God plan in my own strength.

I felt out of alignment, depleted, and ready to give up and settle for a job—something I felt underqualified for after being out of work for so long. I felt like a failure, bustling with activity but financially and spiritually bankrupt.

Then, in my lowest moment, with tears spilling onto a worn-out keyboard, I raised my flag. I surrendered fully: "Lord, I'm tired. I just want to do what You want me to do. I don't care how much money I make, I just want to be in Your perfect will." It was a genuine surrender, and it reached the heavens. As I cried out, a gentle voice whispered, "Go on the Esther fast." It had begun and my plea was accepted and grace was applied.

{POWER PAUSE}

An Esther Fast, drawn from Esther 4, involves three days and nights of fasting, which can bring about victory, expose adversaries, and usher in protection, deliverance, favor, liberty, and freedom. It's a divine interception against the enemy's plans. For those interested, I recommend reading Lenika Scott's book called Fasting For A Breakthrough.

The Reward of Surrender

Emerging from the fast, I was focused, clear-headed, and spiritually renewed. The first divine instruction was shocking yet clear: stop coaching, shut down all programs, halt product sales, and step back from social media. I had claimed to make God the CEO of my venture, but in truth, He was merely a 'glorified board member' whose advice I sought but rarely followed. This realization struck hard.

God showed me that true leadership meant learning to manage what He entrusted to me—starting with His strategies. I had to live out these strategies, become a testament to their efficacy, before I could ever teach them to others.

For two months, God taught me how to surrender to him daily and also how to steward not just business matters but also my family life, which had suffered due to my relentless focus on financial success. This period of recalibration taught me the true essence of submission—not just to God's will but also to the needs of those I loved.

The Life of Surrender

As I mentioned before, Giants in the Gospel with 7 Figure Faith, have unlocked this principle, and discovered that it is a daily practice. Surrendering will reshape your life, your prayer life and open opportunities to a deepend communion with God through fasting.

Your surrender requires a willingness to be led, to obey, and your commitment to your personal process of surrender. There are 3 shifts that will happen in your process of surrendering, it is an immediate shift , a gradual shift, and an eternal shift!

The 3 Shifts After Surrender

The Immediate Shift:

The immediate shift occurs right after your surrender. It's like a burst of divine approval, as heaven celebrates your commitment to aligning with God's plans. This is when you feel a surge of God's spirit, His supernatural power and clarity that rejuvenates your faith and propels you forward.

The Gradual Shift:

As you continue in your surrendered state, you enter a phase of gradual change. Here, God molds and refines you, preparing you to build what He has ordained. This is a time of behind-the-scenes divine orchestration—subtle yet significant alterations that align you closer to your divine purpose.

This is also the time of testing, or as I like to call it, *the breaking and the battle while you build*. It's the moment when the enemy throws his best shot to try to knock the wind out of you; all to get you to STOP building for God's Kingdom purpose. His efforts are not to stop the blessing connected to what you are building, because quite frankly, he can not. However, his goal is to frustrate you enough to forfeit the blessing through pausing or putting off the work of the Lord; the work that will impact millions. He understands that if he can get you to stop obeying God long enough not to build or work on what God said, he can get you to block your own blessing.

It's important to note that during this season, you have to be like Nehemiah, and stay on the wall! Stay consistent. No matter what. When the enemy is aware of you building something that could take down his kingdom, loss is his biggest tactic. You may lose a job, a loved one, or even your home. But stay consistent and remain radically obedient while building/doing what God has instructed you to do. The power of your surrender during this time has to be stronger than your current circumstances. Determine that your circumstances will not be louder than your call!

My Season of Breaking while Building

We were three months into our joint ministry, concurrently battling our property managers in a significant legal dispute. They had locked us out of our rental portal for HOA violations wrongly assigned to us due to an incorrect address. Due to this confusion our funds were tied up in the court and legal fees, but at the start of March 2023, God told us to make our ministry legitimate. With just $147 to our name, we decided that this would be the seed we would invest in getting an LLC and obeying God. It felt good in spite of all we were going through to finally be building something in alignment with our purpose and God's will. Months prior, I had started a prayer call, named First Fruit *prayer call, and began meeting at coffee shops with women to discuss God, the bible, and all things motherhood. Life was life'n in a good way.*

Though He Slay Me

The trial that couldn't break us, came within a week of us celebrating our ministry legitimacy, and right after I finished a message on my youtube channel called Training During Transition. I remember my husband coming into my office and handing me the letter that knocked the wind out of me; a 24 hour mandate to vacate the property.

(LOSS! One of the strongest tactics of the enemy)

I remember trying to console my husband, and the first moment I could get away, I closed myself in my prayer room, and let out a cry that took the sound from my body.

I refused to express defeat, but in between sobs of hyper-ventilating, I vented to God

"Lord, we are always there pouring into so many people, but who has the capacity to pour into us right now?"

God's response was "ME."

An instant strength and soberness fell on me.

At that moment, I picked up a box and began packing. It was nearly midnight when a trusted neighbor noticed our predicament. Seeing our distress, they graciously invited our kids to rest at their place while we finished loading the

U-Haul—a small miracle, considering we had managed to secure one on such short notice. After we wrapped up at 3 AM, they offered us a place to stay. What was supposed to be one night turned into a month of living in their 1600 sq ft three-bedroom home, all seven of us sharing one room, in the couple's home.

Throughout this time, I kept up with the daily prayer calls and even started my publishing company the very next day after the eviction, after God's instruction. Although I didn't have a dollar to my name to get started, I was reminded of the widow with the vessels, and I knew *I had enough oil* to start. Then I heard God promise: "If you take care of my business, I will take care of yours, and you will have a 6 figure launch." And He kept that promise.

This period tested my faith like never before, but it was my surrender and consistency that kept me anchored. I clung to the scriptures, "Though He slay me, yet will I trust Him," and "Stand still and see the salvation of the Lord." To me, standing still didn't mean inactivity; it meant maintaining a posture of surrender, trust, and diligence—staying the course and doing exactly what God had instructed, waiting for His timely intervention.

My friend, this is the power of true surrender—not just enduring trials, but emerging transformed, ready to step into God's promises for your life.This stance requires monumental faith, 7-figure faith, but it's precisely this kind of faith that prepares you for the final and most profound phase of surrender: the eternal shift.

The Eternal Shift

The final phase is the eternal shift. I personally call this *the breakthrough and the blessing*. This comes after you have survived the breaking while managing to thrive in completing the assignment or task God has given you, while you're shifting. This shift causes you to see the long-term fruits of your surrender. It's a profound realignment with God's eternal purposes for you, culminating in breakthroughs and blessings that were orchestrated from the moment of your surrender.

This shift comes as a reward to your diligence and persistence and consistency during the trial of breaking. It's because you didn't waiver in doing your work. During this shift you will experience a MAJOR breakthrough and it will be the thing that establishes the millions for your next move or level with God.

My eternal shift happened over the course of 5 days, but it set the stage for my millions. After 9 months of building with God and being diligent with the prayer call and my now publishing house, God held true to His promise, and during a 5 day challenge, God allowed me to have a 6 figure launch. It was major, and it was mine. Your major breakthrough will come as a result of every time you surrender to God. You have to be confident in knowing that surrendering is the deepest form of submission, and it thereby puts God in total control of His plans for your life. If you can partner with Him in consistency and trust, God will continue to blow your mind and increase your faith.

I pray that this has encouraged you to surrender all and withhold nothing. This cycle of surrender is a necessary principle to apply for each day of your life, towards each new assignment, and definitely at each new level you go to with God. Remember and recognize these shifts, and you will establish the right foundation for the fruit of your 7-figure faith!

To hear more about my first 6 figures testimony, check out my youtube video where I share a bit more in detail. Copy the link in your browser and check it out: https://www.youtube.com/live/mG2fpHl2_Lc?si=ch0R5qpYP9W7fK3o

Faith it Now: Stepping Into Surrender

Let's solidify our learning with actionable steps of how to step into surrendering in this "Faith It Now" section:

To truly surrender:

❧ ***Identify What Holds You Back***:

Reflect on what areas of your life you are holding back from God. Is it your career, relationships, or perhaps your self-esteem?

❧ ***Commit to a Surrender Strategy***:

Whether it's fasting, prayer, or another form of surrender, commit to a strategy that forces you to rely on God's strength rather than your own.

❧ ***Document the Journey***:

Start a journal to document your feelings, revelations, and the changes that occur. This will help you see the tangible benefits of your surrender.

❧ ***Share and Reflect***:

At the end of your commitment period, share your experiences with a trusted friend or mentor. Reflect on how this surrender has shifted your perspective and life.

Embrace these shifts as you surrender to God's will—each one guiding you closer to fulfilling your God-given potential and unlocking your path to 7-figure faith. With each step, you're not just moving towards financial abundance but also towards a life rich in spiritual fulfillment and divine purpose.

CHAPTER 8:

STRUCTURE, SYSTEMS, AND SALES STRATEGY- BUILDING ON SOLID GROUND

Listen, as we near the end of this book, one of the most crucial components of your 7 Figure COMPASS is establishing a solid foundation. We are influential women, called not only to impact and influence but also to generate millions. Remember, God trusts us not only with what we have the faith for but also with what we have the capacity to handle. Recall the story of the widow woman and her vessels.

In this chapter, I want to illuminate the practical aspects of operating and handling millions—emphasizing the importance of having the right systems, structures, and sales strategies in place. To generate income, you must be willing to sell or offer something of value; money must flow towards you before it can be distributed, so understanding sales and the importance of systems is crucial. Remember, God said He gives us the ability to obtain wealth *(Deuteronomy 8:18)*, as well as bless the works of our hands (*Deuteronomy 28:12*). Let's be honest, and accept that the impact and the income will come through working with our ability. The ideas, products, services, and programs God trusts us to bring forth in order to bless in abundance.

When I got this alignment right, everything else was able to fall into place seamlessly, and only then did maintenance and management become routine tasks.

Building Your Business, Ministry, or Profession on Rock

In *Matthew 7:24-27*, Jesus outlines a major difference between two builders: one who builds on rock and another on sand. This parable teaches us about the importance of foundations in life and business. The house built on rock withstands all adversities, while the one on sand collapses under pressure. This metaphor extends perfectly to the realm of business, where the foundation you build—through your structure, systems, and strategy—determines your resilience and success.

The Importance of a Solid Structure

A solid business structure acts like the framework of a house. It supports every other system you implement. For me, aligning my business goals with my spiritual values meant that every decision was rooted in integrity and purpose. This foundational alignment was critical in scaling my business quickly and sustainably.

Learning and Leveraging the Right Systems

Just as a house needs robust plumbing and electrical systems to function smoothly, a business requires effective operational systems to prevent breakdowns and inefficiencies. I learned to implement systems that not only enhanced efficiency but also mirrored Scriptural principles: fostering transparency, accountability, and continuous improvement. The principles I share with you are the same ones I empower my leadership team and authors with, to create significant impact in the marketplace. My proven COMPASS© framework is woven into everything I do and has been pivotal in identifying the right systems and strategies for the success of our business and ministry endeavors.

Honoring God with Our Sales Strategy

While many sales strategies are aggressive and cutthroat, they can also be ethical and compassionate. Inspired by my motivation to truly turn my business affairs over to Christ, and make God the CEO of my business *for real*, I adopted a sales approach focused on honesty, integrity, biblical principals, and service. This approach not only set my business apart in a competitive market but also fostered lasting relationships with clients, proving that integrity does not preclude profitability.

Putting God at the helm as the true CEO of my business transformed me, aligning me with my deepest self-worth—and it can do the same for you. Too often, we shortchange ourselves by undervaluing our services. Remember, our God is a God of grandeur and luxury; after all, the streets of heaven are paved with gold! He desires for your business to reflect the lavish life He envisions for you. Consulting with your divine CEO is essential to understand the full impact of your sales strategy and to ensure it matches the true value and worth you bring to the marketplace.

Mastering the Market: Study, Understand, and Excel

To truly excel in sales, it's imperative to study the market thoroughly and understand who you are serving. This involves more than just knowing the demographics of your target audience—it's about becoming a master in your industry. You need to grasp the nuances of your market's needs and how they evolve. Let the Holy Spirit lead you in all truth as you filter through vast amounts of information. Do not conform to the world's standards or compromise your identity, but tailor this knowledge to fit into your God-given strategy. This alignment ensures that your sales strategies are not only effective but also true to your calling and values.

Sales and Your Seed

"There is no sales strategy that supersedes the power of a seed".
– Apostle Peach

One of the most transformative experiences of my life, marking a capstone moment in operating with 7-Figure Faith, occurred during my very first 5-day challenge. I was fully prepared, with all systems—from email follow-ups to social media and payment processes—set and automated. My week's worth of teachings and videos was queued up and ready to go. I was all set, or so I thought.

Just before the challenge kicked off that Thursday, God imparted a new strategy that completely transformed everything I had planned. Although I was ready to follow the meticulous plan laid out by my Marketing and Sales Coach, God had a switch in store. "Ok God," I chuckled, "I'm all in on Buki's plan, and now you're mixing it up? LOL."

Let me paint the picture for you: I was about to pitch joining my beta group publishing academy for $15k, discounted to $10k for the beta phase. Yet, the true value of what we offered was around $26k. At that point, the most I had ever invested in a program was $15k, and I hadn't yet handled a $20k transaction myself.

God then revealed to me, "You have the potential to be a $50k coach, a $30k speaker, and your one-on-one program is worth $20k, but you haven't sewn into that level of growth yet.

You have the oil for it, but without the seeds to represent that kind of harvest, I can't let you charge that kind of money yet."

He explained that the group of authors joining this challenge would be extraordinary and that if I used this beta launch as a "Jericho Seed," He would consider the contracted agreements as a seed for my future sales and the growth I was anointed to achieve. He set the "seed investment" for the course after the challenge at $7777, emphasizing this was not just a payment but a significant seed of sacrifice and obedience symbolizing the completion of an era for those in the co-hort.

God stressed that this cohort was unlike any before—it was the "Jericho Seed" for me, echoing the story from Joshua 6 about the first city conquered in the Promised Land. Like Joshua, I knew this was my year of entering into my promise, with a six-figure launch prophesied for November. This launch was to be my seed to grow into the wealth mantle and the anointing on my life.

{THE FINAL POWER PAUSE}

I don't know what walls you are facing now, but I speak to every wall of poverty that has tried to keep your treasures trapped, and I command you to SHOUT in this moment for the FREEDOM connected to this next 7 years of victory in your life, business, and ministry! Shout woman of 7-figure Faith! Release it!!!!!

The Completion and Call to 7-figure Anointing

When I wrapped up the challenge after five days, we had garnered $105,000, and by the eighth day, this rose to $116,000 in contracts. God instructed me to allow this group time to cover their costs, launching officially in January 2024. This cohort was not just investing financially; they were planting a Jericho Seed alongside me, accelerating into a future filled with promise, prosperity, and purpose-aligned acceleration.

When I understood that I can have all the right systems, all the right sales tactics, even a divine strategy, but knowing that when I decided to make God the real CEO of my business and ministry, it gave Him the right to disrupt things to do something BETTER! When I realized that I had given God the right to do what was necessary to elevate my destiny, by simply giving Him a seed? I was sold.

This, my friends, is the power of understanding sales as a seed; realizing that no sales strategy can surpass the profound impact of a well-placed seed. If there's one thing I want you to grasp from my journey and this 7-figure faith you're stepping into, as a millionaire, multi-millionaire, deca-millionaire, and even billionaire; it's that your seed is as crucial as your commitment.

Every seed you sow—your words, your time, your finances—matters immensely to God. Your business and your ministry are seeds necessary for activating the 7-figure anointing over your life. Whether it's pricing your services or choosing your sales strategies, bring them before God. Are you pricing based on someone else's blueprint, or are you pricing according to the potential God has shown you?

You may very well be a $1,000 coach or a $1,000,000 coach in the making, but to reach that potential, you must plant seeds that match the harvest you wish to see. Sow where you want to grow.No matter what your services are worth, you have to sow where you are called to grow, and plant seeds based on your potential.

With this in mind, I send you forth to boldly align your faith with the 7-figure anointing on your life and claim your millions. God bless you. It has been an honor to share this journey with you.

The Final Faith it Now: Building Your Blueprint

Let's translate these biblical and business insights into a practical "Faith It Now" action plan:

- ***Reflect on Your Foundation:***

  Assess the current foundation of your business. Is it built on the solid rock of clear values and ethics, or on the shifting sands of opportunism and market trends?

- ***Draft Your Blueprint:***

  Write down key components of your business structure. What are your core values? What systems uphold these values? How does your sales strategy reflect your ethical standards and faith?

- ***Consult the Master Builder:***

  Spend time in prayer, asking God to highlight areas in your business needing restructuring or reinforcement. Seek wisdom for necessary changes and the courage to implement them.

❧ ***Take Action:***

Identify one area built on sand and plan its transformation into a rock-solid component of your business. This might involve enhancing customer service, refining product offerings, or improving marketing ethics.

By engaging with these elements and actively seeking improvement, you align your business with the biblical ideal of building on solid ground. This not only prepares your business to withstand economic storms but also establishes you as a leader who builds with integrity and purpose.

BONUS CHAPTER:
THE OVERFLOW

I was truly moved by reliving the story of what my seed did for me. So much so, I wanted to preach that chapter, LOL! However I definitely wanted to bring out the power in the Jericho seed and prosperity connected to seeds of obedience and sacrifice. So if you are not done with me yet, I have a bit more to the story to add.

The Jericho Seed:
Unlocking Prosperity through Obedience and Sacrifice

The story of Jericho isn't just a tale of conquest; it's a divine blueprint for releasing unprecedented breakthroughs through obedience and sacrifice. Let us tap into the power of Joshua 6, and uncover the strategic and spiritual depths that God orchestrated for His people, a profound lesson that has transformed how I approach my calling and my business.

Joshua 6, verses 1-20 reads:

Now Jericho was straitly shut up because of the children of Israel: none went out, and none came in.

2

And the LORD said unto Joshua, See, I have given into thine hand Jericho, and the king thereof, and the mighty men of valour.

3

And ye shall compass the city, all ye men of war, and go round about the city once. Thus shalt thou do six days.

4

And seven priests shall bear before the ark seven trumpets of rams' horns: and the seventh day ye shall compass the city seven times, and the priests shall blow with the trumpets.

5

And it shall come to pass, that when they make a long blast with the ram's horn, and when ye hear the sound of the trumpet, all the people shall shout with a great shout; and the wall of the city shall fall down flat, and the people shall ascend up every man straight before him.

6

And Joshua the son of Nun called the priests, and said unto them, Take up the ark of the covenant, and let seven priests bear seven trumpets of rams' horns before the ark of the LORD.

7

And he said unto the people, Pass on, and compass the city, and let him that is armed pass on before the ark of the LORD.

8

And it came to pass, when Joshua had spoken unto the people, that the seven priests bearing the seven trumpets of rams' horns passed on before the LORD, and blew with the trumpets: and the ark of the covenant of the LORD followed them.

9

And the armed men went before the priests that blew with the trumpets, and the rereward came after the ark, the priests going on, and blowing with the trumpets.

10

And Joshua had commanded the people, saying, Ye shall not shout, nor make any noise with your voice, neither shall any word proceed out of your mouth, until the day I bid you shout; then shall ye shout.

11

So the ark of the LORD compassed the city, going about it once: and they came into the camp, and lodged in the camp.

12

And Joshua rose early in the morning, and the priests took up the ark of the LORD.

13

And seven priests bearing seven trumpets of rams' horns before the ark of the LORD went on continually, and blew with the trumpets: and the armed men went before them; but the rereward came after the ark of the LORD, the priests going on, and blowing with the trumpets.

14

And the second day they compassed the city once, and returned into the camp: so they did six days.

15

And it came to pass on the seventh day, that they rose early about the dawning of the day, and compassed the city after the same manner seven times: only on that day they compassed the city seven times.

16

And it came to pass at the seventh time, when the priests blew with the trumpets, Joshua said unto the people, Shout; for the LORD hath given you the city.

17

And the city shall be accursed, even it, and all that are therein, to the LORD: only Rahab the harlot shall live, she and all that are with her in the house, because she hid the messengers that we sent.

18

And ye, in any wise keep yourselves from the accursed thing, lest ye make yourselves accursed, when ye take of the accursed thing, and make the camp of Israel a curse, and trouble it.

19

But all the silver, and gold, and vessels of brass and iron, are consecrated unto the LORD: they shall come into the treasury of the LORD.

20

So the people shouted when the priests blew with the trumpets: and it came to pass, when the people heard the sound of the trumpet, and the people shouted with a great shout, that the wall fell down flat, so that the people went up into the city, every man straight before him, and they took the city.

The Battle Plan Unveiled

Jericho was not just any city; it was a fortified stronghold blocking the Israelites' entry into the Promised Land. Its walls were formidable, its warriors fierce, but its fate was sealed by the Lord's command. Joshua, a faithful servant, was given a seemingly unconventional battle plan: march around the city once for six days, and seven times on the seventh day, then shout with all their might. This plan didn't rely on physical weapons but on the power of faith and obedience.

What strikes me most profoundly is the instruction regarding the spoils of Jericho. Unlike typical conquests where victors claim the spoils, here, everything in Jericho was to be consecrated to the Lord—gold, silver, bronze, and iron were to go into the Lord's treasury. This act wasn't just about obedience; it was about honor and sacrifice. Jericho was to be a seed sown back to God, a foundation of trust and submission that would set the stage for Israel's future victories.

Parallel to Modern-Day Entrepreneurship

In my journey, God called for my very own "Jericho Seed." As I prepared for a pivotal business launch, the Lord redirected my strategy, echoing the sacrificial blueprint of Jericho. Just as Joshua was to dedicate the spoils to God, I was instructed to view my business's initial earnings not as profit but as a sacred offering—a seed sown back to God to sanctify the growth and success that were to follow.

This seed was not merely a financial commitment; it was a declaration of dependence. It signified that just as the walls of Jericho fell by divine command, the barriers to my business's prosperity would crumble—not by my hand but through my obedience to God's strategic plan.

The Impact of the Jericho Seed

When Joshua and his people followed through with God's command, not only did Jericho's walls fall, but God's favor was immensely magnified upon Israel. They moved from victory to victory, not because they were strong or numerous but because their obedience aligned them with divine will.

Similarly, the seed I planted at the inception of my business was a testament to my faith in God's provision. It was an investment into the spiritual foundation of my enterprise. By dedicating the initial profits as a seed, I aligned my business under God's rule and authority, trusting that He would multiply it back in ways I couldn't possibly achieve on my own.

A Call to Sacrificial Seed Sowing

The story of Jericho and the principle of the Jericho Seed in my business compel us to reconsider our approach to entrepreneurship. It's an invitation to transform our businesses into platforms of faith-driven impact. When we dedicate our work and its fruits to God, we do more than make a symbolic gesture—we activate a covenant of prosperity that God is eager to honor.

To every entrepreneur reading this: consider your own "Jericho Seed." What are you willing to consecrate back to God as a sign of total surrender and trust? Understand that it's not about the size of the seed but the sincerity of the sacrifice. Just as the walls of Jericho could not withstand the power of divine instruction, no obstacle in your path will stand when you align your business practices with God's perfect will.

By sowing your seed in faith, you are not just investing in your future; you are claiming your place in a lineage of biblical entrepreneurs who understood that true prosperity comes from putting God first. May you become the Joshua of your business , boldly and courageously conquering and mastering the marketplace, allowing every victory to start with a seed of faith, 7-Figure Faith that is.

EPILOGUE:

SEALING YOUR JOURNEY WITH FAITH

As we close the pages of this transformative journey, it's not just an ending—it's a beginning. The seeds have been sown, the foundations laid, and the path illuminated for you, the influential woman called to millions. Through the chapters of this book, we have traveled together, exploring the depth and breadth of what it means to embody a 7 Figure Faith. You have been equipped with the COMPASS framework, each point a stepping stone on your path to spiritual and financial fulfillment.

From Principles to Possibilities

We began with principles, those mustard seed truths that, when nurtured in the fertile soil of faith and action, promise to grow into the abundant life that has been prepared for you. You learned the importance of clarity, of optimizing opportunities through obedience, and of mastering your potential. You discovered how impactful your message could be, learned to navigate the balance between availability and ability, and embraced the power of surrender and submission. Together, we structured strategies and systems designed not just to survive, but to thrive.

Reflect and Rejoice

Now, as you stand on the precipice of what comes next, I invite you to pause and reflect. Reflect on the moments of realization, the challenges that seemed insurmountable but now serve as testimonies to your resilience and faith. Reflect on the widow and her oil, on the builders and their foundations, and see in their stories your own narrative of growth and grace.

Rejoice in the knowledge that you are stepping forward not just with strategies and principles, but with a fortified spirit and a rejuvenated faith. Rejoice, for you are not alone. You walk this path with a network of fellow trailblazers, each a bearer of light and a steward of His manifold grace.

Moving Forward with Faith

As you move from the pages of this book into the reality of your calling, remember that the application of what you have learned is both a daily commitment and a divine adventure. It is an ongoing act of faith, a continuous surrender to the guidance of the Holy Spirit, and a constant endeavor to apply the COMPASS principles to every aspect of your life.

May you find in every day new opportunities to demonstrate your faith through action. May your faith be as dynamic and as real as the challenges you face. May you build not just a legacy of wealth but a testament to the transformative power of living a life fully aligned with His will.

A Prayer for Your Journey

Lord, bless the reader who has journeyed through these pages. Equip her with courage, fortify her with wisdom, and envelop her in Your unconditional love. Let her steps be bold and her heart be brave as she applies the teachings she has gleaned. Multiply her influence, expand her territory, and let her impact be a monument of Your love and power.

And now, to you, the architect of a future filled with promise and purpose: Go forth with the assurance that what God has begun in you, He will faithfully complete. Your journey continues, and the best is yet to come.

Amen.

HIRE TAUSHAUNA BURREL FOR YOUR NEXT EVENT

Corporate Events - Leadership Development

Taushauna Burrel brings her expertise in leadership development, and 20 years of sales experience to your next corporate event. Her keynote speech focuses on vital topics tailored to high-performing women and sales professionals.

Taushauna's Signature Talk, "The Price of Leadership" is a powerful and igniting presentation for professionals at any level. Attendees will leave with enhanced skills in:

- ***Empowering Leadership:*** Learn how to inspire and influence with integrity and authenticity.
- ***Strategic Storytelling:*** Master the art of storytelling to elevate your brand and leadership presence.
- ***Navigating Corporate Challenges:*** Gain insights into overcoming obstacles with resilience and strategic planning.
- A copy of her inspiration and empowering book for leaders "7-Figure Leaders"

The benefits of Taushauna's presentations are profound, offering lasting impact through improved leadership effectiveness and increased sales performance. Contracts for hire include a negotiated number of her books for attendees, adding value to the learning experience.

Faith-Based or Empowerment Events

For faith-based or empowerment gatherings, Taushauna delivers her signature talk, "7 Figure Faith." This powerful presentation dives into:

- ***Activating Faith:*** Strategies for integrating faith into professional endeavors for miraculous outcomes.
- ***Living Authentically:*** Encouragement to lead lives that fully embody one's faith and professional goals.

- ***Empowerment to Achieve:*** Motivation for attendees to reach their pinnacle of success in both personal and professional spheres.

Entrepreneurial Seminars, Workshops, and Panels

Taushauna is well-equipped to lead seminars, workshops, and panel discussions on a broad array of topics suitable for entrepreneurs at any stage of their business journey. She is known for her ability to activate and ignite purpose and confidence in her audience. Possible topics include:

- ***From Ministry to Mogul:*** Transitioning from faith-based initiatives to substantial business ventures.
- ***Crafting Your Story:*** How to tell your story to inspire, connect, and elevate your entrepreneurial journey.
- ***Mastering Media Relations:*** Techniques for getting your message out through premium media outlets.
- ***Unlocking Your Potential:*** Strategies for identifying and leveraging your unique strengths in the marketplace.
- ***Innovative Income Streams:*** How to diversify and create multiple streams of revenue effectively.

Taushauna's dynamic presence and profound insights provide immense benefits, inspiring audiences to enact real change and harness their full potential.

For more information and to discuss potential engagements, please visit Taushauna Burrel's official website https://www.taushaunaburrel.com/contact or reach out to booking@taushaunaburrel.com.

Here, you can also inquire about her availability and explore how her talks can be tailored to meet the unique needs of your audience.

WE LOVE HEARING FROM YOU: SHARE YOUR JOURNEY & TESTIMONIALS

Your Voice Matters

As you journey through "7 Figure Faith" and begin implementing its principles, your experiences, insights, and breakthroughs are invaluable. We cherish your stories and feedback, and we believe they inspire and encourage others just like you.

Share Your Testimonial

Have you experienced a transformation? Has "7 Figure Faith" helped you ascend to new heights in your personal and professional life? We want to hear about it! Your story could be the beacon that lights the way for others navigating their path to 7-figure faith.

How to Submit Your Testimonial

Submitting your testimonial is easy! Just follow these simple steps:

- ***Write Your Story:***
  Take a moment to write down your journey. How has "7 Figure Faith" impacted you? What changes have you noticed in your life and work? How are you using the insights from the book to shape your future?
- ***Visit Our Submission Page:***
  Go to www.taushaunaburrel.com/testimonials to submit your story. Fill out the form with your name, contact information, and testimonial. You can also upload a video if you'd prefer to share your story visually and send it to admin@taushaunaburrel.com
- ***Submit and Share:***
  Once you've filled out the form, hit submit. We'd love for you to also share your story on social media in our group with the hashtag #7FigureFaithJourney. Let's spread the word and inspire a movement!

Reviews Are Welcome

Loved "7 Figure Faith"? Please consider leaving a review on Amazon, Goodreads, or in our facebook community with #myreview. Your reviews not only help us improve but also help other potential readers understand the powerful impact this book can have on their lives.

Featured Testimonials

Every month, we select impactful testimonials to feature on our website and across our social media platforms. Sharing your experience can profoundly affect others and potentially get your story featured, providing you with a platform to showcase your success and inspire others.
Why Your Testimonials Matter

Your testimonials:

- Inspire others to take the leap into their 7-figure faith journey.
- Provide real-life examples of how the principles in the book apply to various circumstances.
- Help us improve future editions of the book and other resources we offer.

Thank You for Being Part of Our Community

Your insights and stories are what make this journey so rewarding. Thank you for choosing to walk this path with us and for sharing your progress. Together, we are not just dreaming of a better future; we are making it a reality.

Submit Your Testimonial

Let's continue to grow together and make the 7-figure faith a universal beacon of success and spiritual fulfillment.

DISCOVER THE COMPANION BOOK TO TRANSFORM YOUR JOURNEY: "7 FIGURE LEADERS"

For the Woman of Influence: Cultivating an Environment for Success

As you close the last page of "7 Figure Faith," your journey is just beginning. Extend your path to success and leadership with our essential companion guide, "7 Figure Leaders"—specifically crafted for women of influence and professionals ready to cultivate a thriving environment for leadership.

Why "7 Figure Leaders"?

Our companion book is more than just a follow-up—it's a blueprint for building your legacy. "7 Figure Leaders" is designed to help you:

- ***Deepen Your Understanding:*** Explore advanced strategies and insights that complement and expand upon the teachings of "7 Figure Faith."
- ***Implement with Precision:*** Find actionable steps to apply the principles directly to your professional and spiritual life, ensuring you build a robust framework for success.
- ***Network with High Achievers:*** Learn how to identify, attract, and foster relationships with other high-performing individuals in your industry and beyond.

What's Inside?

"7 Figure Leaders" is packed with tools and techniques tailored for the ambitious female leader:

- ***Leadership Blueprints:*** Detailed guides on structuring your business and ministry to foster growth and scalability.
- ***Advanced Prayer Strategies:*** Deeper spiritual insights to align your purpose with God's plan at higher levels of responsibility.
- ***Case Studies and Testimonials:*** Inspirational stories from women who have successfully transitioned from ministry to mogul.

Exclusive Offer Just for You

As a reader of "7 Figure Faith," we are excited to offer you "7 Figure Leaders" at an exclusive discounted rate. But that's not all—by purchasing this companion guide, you will also gain access to our private Facebook community of 7 Figure Faith'ers, where you can network, share, and learn with a supportive group of like-minded leaders.

Special Bonuses

- ***Monthly Giveaways:*** New members can win exciting prizes each month, enhancing your journey with both spiritual and practical rewards.
- ***Annual $1,000 Draw:*** Stay active in the community for a chance to win our grand annual giveaway, a testament to our commitment to your success.

Take the Next Step

Are you ready to elevate your influence and secure your spot as a 7 Figure Leader? Click the link below to purchase your copy of "7 Figure Leaders" and transform your potential into power.

Buy "7 Figure Leaders" Now

Join us, and let's make your 7-figure dream a reality, together.

ACKNOWLEDGMENTS

Writing this book has been a journey of profound transformation, not only for me but for everyone involved in bringing "7-Figure Faith" to life. I am immensely grateful to my family, whose unwavering support and love provide the foundation upon which my work is built. To my husband, who has been a pillar of strength and encouragement, nurturing my dreams alongside his own.

I extend heartfelt thanks to the incredible team at 120 Publishing House, whose expertise and dedication have turned raw manuscripts into powerful messages that reach hearts and minds across the globe. A special thank you to my editor, whose keen eye and insightful feedback have sharpened the words on these pages.

To my spiritual mentors and the community of faith that surrounds me, your guidance and prayers have been indispensable. Your wisdom has been a compass during moments of doubt and uncertainty.

And to you, my readers, who inspire me to share my journey and insights—thank you for embracing this work. Your stories of triumph and perseverance motivate me to continue writing and teaching.

May this book serve as a testament to what is possible when faith meets action, and may it empower you to seize the abundance that awaits.

ABOUT THE AUTHOR

Taushauna Burrel is an international speaker, founder of 120 Publishing House, and a visionary leader who specializes in transforming Christian women with corporate experience into moguls called to nations.

Through her elite agency, Taushauna empowers these women to prophesy through pages with powerful storytelling and prepares them to take their message to premium media outlets.

As a testament to her calling, Taushauna authored "7 Figure Faith," a guide for those ready to activate their faith and ascend to their God-given potential in the marketplace. To extend this journey, she invites you to visit her website at taushaunaburrel.com, where you can explore more resources, book a personal call with her, or grab a special gift—a downloadable eBook companion, "7 Figure Leaders."

Join her transformative community today and get a chance to win in our $1,000 yearly and monthly drawing by joining our Facebook groups. Each member not only gains access to an empowering network but also the collective wisdom shared within these vibrant spaces.

ARE YOU CALLED TO PROPHESY THROUGH PAGES?

Do you feel a deep-seated call to deliver a message to millions? Are you destined to dominate a mountain of influence, using powerful storytelling to glorify the Kingdom and impact nations? If your heart says "yes," then we have something special for you.

Accept This Gift from 120 Publishing House

We understand the journey to turning ministry into moguldom isn't just a path but a divine assignment. To support you on this transformative venture, 120 Publishing House is delighted to offer you a unique gift designed to propel you forward in your mission. Leverage our expertise to amplify your voice and make your mark in the world.

Embrace your calling, enrich your mission, and engage with the masses. Click or copy the link below or scan the QR code to begin your journey to making a monumental impact today.

Accept Your Gift and Start Your Journey

Scan Code or You can get a copy by visiting:
https://www.taushaunaburrel.com/finisher-guide-1

www.ingramcontent.com/pod-product-compliance
Lightning Source LLC
LaVergne TN
LVHW010926110826
845149LV00013B/2493

* 9 7 9 8 9 8 9 2 8 0 6 4 3 *